# JavaScript Handbook Object-Oriented Programming (OOP)

Mastering Object-Oriented Programming with JavaScript: A Hands-on Approach

By
Laurence Lars Svekis

**For more content and to learn more, visit**
https://basescripts.com/

# JavaScript Handbook Object-Oriented Programming (OOP)

## Table of Contents

# Summary

The **JavaScript Handbook: Object-Oriented Programming (OOP)** provides a comprehensive guide to mastering OOP concepts in JavaScript. It starts with foundational principles like objects, constructors, and prototypes before progressing to advanced concepts like inheritance, polymorphism, and encapsulation.
Through clear explanations, coding exercises, and multiple-choice questions, readers gain hands-on experience and insight

into building maintainable, scalable applications. Each chapter introduces a key OOP concept, explains how it works in practice, and challenges readers with real-world scenarios. Topics like method chaining, mixins, and ES6 classes are covered in depth.

By the end of the book, readers will have a solid foundation in OOP principles and the confidence to apply them to modern web development, particularly in frameworks like React, Vue.js, and Angular. The skills learned in this book are essential for building robust applications and understanding the underlying structure of modern JavaScript.

# Introduction

Welcome to the **JavaScript Handbook: Object-Oriented Programming (OOP)**. This book is your ultimate guide to mastering one of the most essential concepts in modern JavaScript development. Whether you're a beginner taking your first steps into the world of OOP or an experienced developer looking to refine your skills, this book provides a structured path to deep understanding.

Object-oriented programming (OOP) is at the heart of many software development paradigms. It powers everything from modern frameworks to large-scale applications. By mastering OOP, you'll be equipped to build scalable, maintainable, and efficient software.

This handbook begins with foundational concepts like objects and constructors, gradually leading you into advanced topics like inheritance, polymorphism, encapsulation, and method chaining. Each chapter includes theory, hands-on coding exercises, multiple-choice questions with explanations, and detailed solutions. You'll learn not only *how* to write OOP-style code, but also *why* it matters.

Expect to build practical skills that you can immediately apply to your projects. By the end of this book, you'll have a solid grasp of OOP, which is essential for working with frameworks, libraries, and large-scale applications.

Get ready to take your JavaScript development skills to the next level. Let's dive in!

# JavaScript Objects

## Introduction to Objects

In JavaScript, objects are collections of key-value pairs. They are one of the most fundamental data types, enabling you to store, manipulate, and organize complex data. Almost everything in JavaScript (strings, numbers, arrays, functions) can be wrapped in an object form, and objects form the building blocks of the language's powerful features.

## Creating Objects

**Object Literals**: The most common way to create an object is using curly braces {} and defining properties inside them.
```
const person = {
   name: "Alice",
   age: 30
};
```
**Using new Object()**:
```
const obj = new Object();
obj.key = "value";
```
**Constructor Functions and Classes**: More advanced ways to create objects.

## Object Properties

**Properties** are key-value pairs. The key is usually a string (or Symbol), and the value can be any type: string, number, boolean, array, function, or another object.
```
const car = {
   brand: "Toyota",
   model: "Corolla",
   year: 2020,
   color: "blue"
```

```
};
```
- **Accessing Properties**:
  - ○ Dot notation: `car.brand`
  - ○ Bracket notation: `car["model"]`

**Modifying and Adding Properties**:
```
car.color = "red";
car.owner = "Alice"; // added new property
```
**Deleting Properties**:
```
delete car.year;
```

## Object Methods

**Methods** are properties that hold function values. They allow objects to have behavior.
```
const mathOperations = {
  x: 10,
  y: 5,
  add: function() {
    return this.x + this.y;
  },
  multiply() {
    return this.x * this.y;
  }
};
console.log(mathOperations.add());      // 15
console.log(mathOperations.multiply()); // 50
```
- Notice the use of `this` to refer to the current object's properties.
- From ES6 onward, you can define methods without the `function` keyword.

## Property Descriptors and Object Methods

JavaScript provides built-in methods like `Object.keys()`, `Object.values()`, and `Object.entries()` for iterating over object properties:
```
const user = { name: "John", age: 25 };
```

```
console.log(Object.keys(user));    // ["name",
"age"]
console.log(Object.values(user)); // ["John",
25]
console.log(Object.entries(user)); // [["name",
"John"], ["age", 25]]
```

## Object Copying and Reference

Objects are reference types. Assigning one object to another
variable does not create a copy; it creates a reference.
```
const original = { a: 1 };
const copy = original;
copy.a = 2;
console.log(original.a); // 2 (both point to
the same object)
```
- To create a shallow copy:

Use `Object.assign()`:
```
const shallowCopy = Object.assign({},
original);
```
Use the spread operator:
```
const shallowCopy2 = { ...original };
```

## Checking Properties

in operator:
```
if ("name" in user) console.log("user has a
name");
```
hasOwnProperty() method:
```
user.hasOwnProperty("age"); // true
```

# Multiple Choice Questions (With Answers and Explanations)

1. How do you create an object literal in JavaScript?
A. `const obj = {};`
B. `const obj = new Object();`
C. `const obj = new {};`
D. `const obj = ();`
**Answer: A**
**Explanation:** `{}` is the literal syntax for creating an object.
2. Which of these is a valid object property access using dot notation?
A. `obj["key"]`
B. `obj.key`
C. `obj(key)`
D. `obj->key`
**Answer: B**
**Explanation:** Dot notation uses `obj.key`.
3. If `const car = {brand: "Ford"}; const anotherCar = car; anotherCar.brand = "Toyota";` What is `car.brand`?
A. "Ford"
B. "Toyota"
C. undefined
D. ReferenceError
**Answer: B**
**Explanation:** Both `car` and `anotherCar` reference the same object.
4. How to delete a property age from `person` object?
A. `remove person.age;`
B. `person.age = undefined;`
C. `delete person.age;`
D. `person.clear(age);`
**Answer: C**
**Explanation:** The `delete` operator removes a property from an object.
5. To check if property "name" exists in `user`, which is correct?
A. `"name" in user`
B. `user.hasOwn("name")`
C. `propertyExists(user.name)`

D. typeof user.name === "exists"
**Answer: A**
**Explanation:** "propertyName" in object checks property existence.
6. Which method returns an array of keys of an object?
A. Object.keys(obj)
B. Object.values(obj)
C. Object.entries(obj)
D. Object.getKeys(obj)
**Answer: A**
**Explanation:** Object.keys() returns an array of the object's keys.
7. In an object method, this refers to:
A. The global object
B. The object the method is called on
C. Always window
D. this is undefined in methods
**Answer: B**
**Explanation:** In a method, this refers to the object itself.
8. What is the result of Object.values({x:10,y:20})?
A. ["x","y"]
B. [10,20]
C. [["x",10],["y",20]]
D. {x:10,y:20}
**Answer: B**
**Explanation:** Object.values() returns an array of property values.
9. Object.entries(user) returns:
A. An array of keys
B. An array of values
C. An array of [key, value] pairs
D. A single value
**Answer: C**
**Explanation:** Object.entries() returns an array of [key, value] arrays.

9

10. What does `Object.assign(target, source)` do?
A. Merges properties of source into target, returning target
B. Creates a deep clone of source
C. Deletes properties from target
D. Does nothing
**Answer: A**
**Explanation:** `Object.assign()` copies properties from source to target.

11. How can you define a method inside an object from ES6 onward without `function` keyword?
A. `method() { ... }`
B. `function method() {...}`
C. `:method = () => {}`
D. `~method() {...}`
**Answer: A**
**Explanation:** Shorthand method definition: `methodName() { ... }`.

12. Which operator checks if "prop" is a property of obj?
A. `obj.prop`
B. `"prop" in obj`
C. `prop in obj` (without quotes)
D. `obj.hasProperty(prop)`
**Answer: B**
**Explanation:** `"prop" in obj` checks property existence.

13. What does `delete obj.key;` return if key existed?
A. `true`
B. `false`
C. `undefined`
D. It throws an error
**Answer: A**
**Explanation:** `delete` returns `true` if the property was successfully deleted.

14. If `const person = {name:"Bob"};`
`person.age=25;` what is `person` after these operations?
A. `{name:"Bob"}`
B. `{name:"Bob", age:25}`
C. `{name:"Bob", age:undefined}`

D. Throws error
**Answer: B**
**Explanation:** Adding a property just adds it: {name:"Bob", age:25}.

15.  Which statement about objects is true?
A. Object keys must be numbers
B. Object keys are always converted to strings
C. You cannot add properties after creation
D. Objects are immutable
**Answer: B**
**Explanation:** Keys in objects are strings (or Symbols), numeric keys become strings.

16.  If you do const a = {}; const b = a; and then b.newProp = 123; what's in a?
A. {}
B. {newProp:123}
C. undefined
D. {newProp:undefined}
**Answer: B**
**Explanation:** a and b reference the same object, so a shows the new property.

17.  hasOwnProperty() checks if:
A. The object has the property defined directly on it, not in the prototype chain
B. The object has the property anywhere in the prototype chain
C. The property value is not null
D. The property key is numeric
**Answer: A**
**Explanation:** hasOwnProperty() checks directly on the object, not inherited properties.

18.  To create a shallow copy of an object, which syntax is correct?
A. const copy = {...original};
B. const copy = *original;
C. const copy = original;
D. const copy = original.clone();
**Answer: A**

**Explanation:** Spread syntax {...original} creates a shallow copy.

19. If you console.log(Object.keys({a:1,b:2})), what is output?

A. {a:1,b:2}

B. ["1","2"]

C. ["a","b"]

D. [["a",1],["b",2]]

**Answer: C**

**Explanation:** Object.keys() returns ["a","b"].

20. Object.freeze(obj) does what?

A. Deletes all properties

B. Prevents adding, removing, or changing properties

C. Only prevents adding new properties

D. Returns a new object

**Answer: B**

**Explanation:** Object.freeze() makes the object immutable.

# 10 Coding Exercises with Full Solutions and Explanations

## 1. Create and Access Object Properties

**Problem:**
Create an object book with properties title and author. Log the title using dot notation.

**Solution:**
```
const book = {
  title: "1984",
  author: "George Orwell"
};
console.log(book.title); // "1984"
```
**Explanation:**
We defined an object literal and accessed a property using dot notation.

## 2. Add and Delete Properties

**Problem:**
Create an object `car` with `brand` = "Honda". Add a property `model` = `"Civic"` and then delete `brand`. Log the resulting object.

**Solution:**
```
const car = { brand: "Honda" };
car.model = "Civic";
delete car.brand;
console.log(car); // { model: "Civic" }
```
**Explanation:**
We added `model` and then removed `brand`, leaving `{model:"Civic"}`.

## 3. Object Method Using this

**Problem:**
Create an object `calculator` with properties a=5, b=3, and a method sum that returns a+b. Log the result of `calculator.sum()`.

**Solution:**
```
const calculator = {
  a: 5,
  b: 3,
  sum() {
    return this.a + this.b;
  }
};
console.log(calculator.sum()); // 8
```
**Explanation:**
Method uses `this` to access object's properties.

## 4. Check Property Existence

**Problem:**
Create `user = { name: "Alice", age: 25 }`. Check if age is in `user` and log "Has age" if true.
**Solution:**
```
const user = { name: "Alice", age: 25 };
if ("age" in user) {
  console.log("Has age"); // "Has age"
}
```
**Explanation:**
`"age" in user` returns true, so we log "Has age".

## 5. Iterate Over Object Keys

**Problem:**
Given `const obj = {x:10,y:20,z:30}`, use `Object.keys` and a loop to log each key and its value.
**Solution:**
```
const obj = { x: 10, y: 20, z: 30 };
const keys = Object.keys(obj);
for (let key of keys) {
  console.log(key, obj[key]);
}
// x 10
// y 20
// z 30
```
**Explanation:**
We loop over keys and access values with bracket notation.

## 6. Object.values Example

**Problem:**
Given `const fruit = { apple: 2, banana: 5 };` log the values array using `Object.values()`.
**Solution:**
```
const fruit = { apple: 2, banana: 5 };
console.log(Object.values(fruit)); // [2,5]
```

**Explanation:**
`Object.values()` returns `[2,5]`.

## 7. Object.entries Example

**Problem:**
Given `const settings = { theme: "dark", language: "en" };` use `Object.entries()` and a for-of loop to log key-value pairs.
**Solution:**
```
const settings = { theme: "dark", language: "en" };
for (const [key, value] of
Object.entries(settings)) {
  console.log(key, value);
}
// theme dark
// language en
```
**Explanation:**
`Object.entries()` returns
`[["theme","dark"],["language","en"]]`.

## 8. Copy Object Using Spread

**Problem:**
Make a shallow copy of `const original = {a:1, b:2}` into copy and change `copy.b=3` without affecting `original`.
**Solution:**
```
const original = { a: 1, b: 2 };
const copy = { ...original };
copy.b = 3;
console.log(original.b); // 2
console.log(copy.b);     // 3
```

**Explanation:**
Spread syntax creates a new object. Changing `copy` doesn't affect `original`.

## 9. Using hasOwnProperty()

**Problem:**
Check if book has its own property "title" using hasOwnProperty.
**Solution:**
```
const book = { title: "Invisible Man", author: "Ralph Ellison" };
console.log(book.hasOwnProperty("title")); // true
```
**Explanation:**
`hasOwnProperty("title")` returns true.

## 10. Adding a Method That Modifies an Object

**Problem:**
Create person = {name:"Bob", greet() {console.log("Hello "+this.name);}}. Call person.greet(). Then change person.name="Charlie" and call person.greet() again.
**Solution:**
```
const person = {
  name: "Bob",
  greet() {
    console.log("Hello " + this.name);
  }
};
person.greet(); // "Hello Bob"
person.name = "Charlie";
person.greet(); // "Hello Charlie"
```
**Explanation:**
The method uses `this.name`, so changing name updates the greeting.

# Conclusion

Objects are central to JavaScript, allowing you to store key-value pairs, define methods, and model complex data and behavior. Understanding how to create, access, modify, and iterate over objects, as well as how to use methods like `Object.keys()`, `Object.values()`, and `Object.entries()`, is fundamental. By mastering these concepts, you can structure your code more effectively and create robust data models within your JavaScript applications.

# JavaScript Object Constructors

## Introduction

In JavaScript, objects can be created using object literals, but for situations where you need to create multiple similar objects with shared structure and behaviors, object constructors are a powerful solution. Constructors allow you to define a blueprint for objects, making code more organized and maintainable.

## What is a Constructor?

A **constructor** is typically a function that initializes an object's properties. When called with the new keyword, the function returns a new object instance linked to the constructor's prototype.

**Key points:**
- Constructors are capitalized by convention to distinguish them from regular functions.
- The new keyword creates a new object, sets its prototype, and binds `this` to the new object.

## Constructor Functions (Pre-ES6)

**Example:**

```
function Person(name, age) {
  this.name = name;
  this.age = age;
  this.greet = function() {
    console.log("Hello, my name is " +
this.name);
  };
}
const alice = new Person("Alice", 30);
alice.greet(); // "Hello, my name is Alice"
```
**How it works:**
1. new Person("Alice", 30) creates a new empty object.
2. this inside Person is bound to the new object.
3. Properties (this.name, this.age) and methods
(this.greet) are set on the new object.
4. The newly created object is returned.

## Adding Methods to the Prototype

To avoid recreating methods for each instance, you can add
methods to the constructor's prototype. This improves memory
efficiency.
```
function Person(name, age) {
  this.name = name;
  this.age = age;
}
Person.prototype.greet = function() {
  console.log("Hello, I'm " + this.name);
};
const bob = new Person("Bob", 25);
bob.greet(); // "Hello, I'm Bob"
```
Now, all Person instances share the greet method from the
prototype.

## Built-in Constructors

JavaScript provides built-in constructors like `Object`, `Array`, `Date`, RegExp, etc.

```
const arr = new Array(1, 2, 3); // Not
recommended, prefer literals: [1,2,3]
```

While you can use built-in constructors, it's often more readable to use literals.

## ES6 Classes (Syntactic Sugar)

ES6 introduced the `class` keyword, which is syntactic sugar over prototype-based constructors.

```
class Person {
  constructor(name, age) {
    this.name = name;
    this.age = age;
  }
  greet() {
    console.log(`Hi, I'm ${this.name}`);
  }
}
const charlie = new Person("Charlie", 40);
charlie.greet(); // "Hi, I'm Charlie"
```

Classes make constructor-based object creation more familiar and organized, but under the hood, they use prototypes.

## Factory Functions vs Constructors

Alternatively, you can create functions that return objects without using new. These are called factory functions, which can be simpler, but lack `instanceof` checks naturally tied to constructors.

```
function createPerson(name, age) {
  return {
    name,
    age,
```

```
    greet() {
        console.log(`Hello, ${this.name}`);
    }
  };
}
const dave = createPerson("Dave", 20);
dave.greet();
```
Both patterns are valid; choose based on your needs.

# Multiple Choice Questions (With Answers and Explanations)

1. Which keyword is used to create a new object instance from a constructor function? A. `create` B. `class` C. new D. `instance`

**Answer: C**

**Explanation:** new creates a new instance of a constructor function.

2. By convention, constructor function names: A. Are lowercase
B. Start with an uppercase letter
C. Must start with _
D. Are always called `Constructor`

**Answer: B**

**Explanation:** Constructor names usually start with uppercase to distinguish them.

3. In a constructor function, this refers to: A. The global object
B. The instance being created
C. The constructor function itself
D. undefined

**Answer: B**

**Explanation:** In a constructor, this refers to the newly created instance.

Which of the following creates an object using a constructor?
```
function Car(make) {
    this.make = make;
}
```

4. A. `Car("Toyota")`
B. `new Car("Toyota")`
C. `Car.new("Toyota")`
D. `new Object(Car("Toyota"))`
**Answer: B**
**Explanation:** `new Car("Toyota")` correctly creates a new object instance.
5. If you forget to use new when calling a constructor: A. It still creates a new instance
B. `this` will not refer to the new object
C. It throws a SyntaxError
D. It automatically fixes itself
**Answer: B**
**Explanation:** Without new, `this` refers to undefined in strict mode, or global object in sloppy mode, not the intended new object.
6. Where should you define methods to avoid recreating them for each instance? A. Inside the constructor on `this`
B. On the constructor's prototype
C. On a global variable
D. In a separate function not related to the constructor
**Answer: B**
**Explanation:** Defining methods on the prototype saves memory and is more efficient.
7. Using ES6 classes: A. Replaces the prototype chain mechanism entirely
B. Is just syntactic sugar over constructor functions and prototypes
C. Doesn't allow using new
D. Involves no prototypes
**Answer: B**
**Explanation:** Classes in ES6 are syntactic sugar over the existing prototype-based inheritance.
8. The `instanceof` operator checks: A. If an object was created by a particular constructor
B. If the object has a specific property
C. If the object is a function

D. If the object is frozen
**Answer: A**
**Explanation:** `instanceof` checks the constructor in an object's prototype chain.
9. Which is a benefit of using constructors? A. Easier to clone objects without reference
B. Consistent structure for similar objects
C. Automatic memory management
D. No need for prototypes
**Answer: B**
**Explanation:** Constructors provide a blueprint for creating objects with the same structure.
10.   How do you add a method to all instances created by a constructor? A. `ConstructorName.method = function(){}`

B. `ConstructorName.prototype.method = function(){}`

C. `ConstructorName.__proto__.method = function(){}`

D. `new ConstructorName().method = function(){}`
**Answer: B**
**Explanation:** Adding a method to `ConstructorName.prototype` affects all instances.
11.   If `const user = new Person("John",30);`, how do you check if `user` was created by `Person`? A. `user.constructor === Person`
B. `user instanceof Person`
C. `typeof user === "Person"`
D. `user.class === "Person"`
**Answer: B**
**Explanation:** `user instanceof Person` returns true if Person is in the prototype chain.
12.   If a constructor doesn't return anything: A. It returns `undefined`
B. It returns the newly created object by default
C. It throws an error
D. It returns `this` if no return statement
**Answer: B**

**Explanation:** A constructor called with new returns the new object implicitly if no other object is returned.

13.  Can a constructor return a different object? A. No, that's not allowed

B. Yes, if you return an object explicitly, that object is returned instead of the new instance

C. Only with strict mode

D. Only in ES6 classes

**Answer: B**

**Explanation:** If a constructor returns an object, that object becomes the result of new.

14.  To prevent accidental omission of new in a constructor call, you can: A. Check if this is an instance of the constructor and correct it

B. Use use strict mode to fix automatically

C. Write a factory function instead of a constructor

D. Throw an error if this is not an instance

**Answer: D**

**Explanation:** Common pattern: if this is not instance of the constructor, throw an error.

15.  In ES6 classes, which method is called when creating a new instance? A. build()

B. constructor()

C. init()

D. new()

**Answer: B**

**Explanation:** The constructor() method is executed on new in ES6 classes.

16.  The prototype property of a constructor function is: A. An array of all instances

B. An object shared by all instances for shared methods/properties

C. The constructor itself

D. A private property not accessible

**Answer: B**

**Explanation:** ConstructorFunction.prototype is used for shared methods.

17.  new Object() is typically not recommended because: A. It's slower than literals
B. It doesn't create a new object
C. It's not valid syntax
D. Literals ({}) are more concise and clear
**Answer: D**
**Explanation:** Object literals are shorter and more readable.
18.  A factory function differs from a constructor in that: A. Factory doesn't use new
B. Factory must use new
C. Constructors can't have methods
D. Factories can't return an object
**Answer: A**
**Explanation:** Factory functions return objects without using new.
19.  If person.prototype is modified, who sees the change? A. Only new instances
B. All existing and new instances
C. No one, prototype changes are ignored
D. Only the instance currently in use
**Answer: B**
**Explanation:** Changes to the prototype are reflected in all instances referencing that prototype.
20.  In an ES6 class, methods defined inside constructor() on this are: A. Shared by all instances
B. Created anew for each instance
C. Automatically placed on the prototype
D. Not allowed
**Answer: B**
**Explanation:** Methods defined on this inside constructor are instance-specific, not shared.

# 10 Coding Exercises with Full Solutions and Explanations

## 1. Basic Constructor Function

**Problem:** Create a constructor function `Car` that takes `brand` and `model` and stores them. Create a new instance and log its properties.
**Solution:**
```
function Car(brand, model) {
  this.brand = brand;
  this.model = model;
}
const myCar = new Car("Toyota", "Corolla");
console.log(myCar.brand); // "Toyota"
console.log(myCar.model); // "Corolla"
```
**Explanation:**
`Car` sets `this.brand` and `this.model`. Using `new Car(...)` creates a new object with those properties.

## 2. Add a Method via Prototype

**Problem:** Add a method `getInfo()` to `Car` prototype that returns "brand model".
**Solution:**
```
Car.prototype.getInfo = function() {
  return this.brand + " " + this.model;
};
console.log(myCar.getInfo()); // "Toyota Corolla"
```
**Explanation:**
Methods on the prototype are shared. No duplication per instance.

## 3. Check Instance

**Problem:** Use `instanceof` to check if `myCar` is an instance of `Car`.
**Solution:**
```
console.log(myCar instanceof Car); // true
```

**Explanation:**
`instanceof` returns true because `myCar` was created by `Car`.

## 4. Return a Different Object from Constructor

**Problem:** Modify `Car` constructor to return a different object if `brand` is "Ford".
**Solution:**
```
function Car(brand, model) {
   if (brand === "Ford") {
     return { brand: "Ford", model: model,
special: true };
   }
   this.brand = brand;
   this.model = model;
}
const specialCar = new Car("Ford", "Fiesta");
console.log(specialCar); // {brand:"Ford",
model:"Fiesta", special:true}
```
**Explanation:**
Constructor returns a different object, which overrides the normal `this` return.

## 5. ES6 Class Constructor

**Problem:** Create a `class Person` with `constructor(name, age)` and a method `sayHello()` that logs "Hello from name". Create an instance and call `sayHello()`.
**Solution:**
```
class Person {
   constructor(name, age) {
     this.name = name;
     this.age = age;
   }
   sayHello() {
     console.log("Hello from " + this.name);
   }
```

```
}
const p = new Person("Alice", 30);
p.sayHello(); // "Hello from Alice"
```
**Explanation:**
ES6 classes provide a clean syntax for constructors and
methods.

## 6. Shared Method vs Instance Method

**Problem:** In a constructor Gadget, define a function on this
and another on Gadget.prototype. Compare memory usage
(not actually measured, just commented in code).
**Solution:**
```
function Gadget(name) {
  this.name = name;
  this.showName = function() {
    return "Instance method: " + this.name;
  };
}
Gadget.prototype.showType = function() {
  return "Prototype method shared by all
instances";
};
const g1 = new Gadget("Phone");
const g2 = new Gadget("Tablet");
console.log(g1.showName === g2.showName); //
false (unique functions)
console.log(g1.showType === g2.showType); //
true (shared function)
```
**Explanation:**
showName is recreated for each instance, while showType is
shared.

## 7. Using constructor property

27

**Problem:** Check the `constructor` property of an instance to see which constructor function was used.
**Solution:**
```
console.log(myCar.constructor === Car); // true
```
**Explanation:**
Every instance has a `constructor` property referencing its constructor function.

## 8. Add Property After Instances Are Created

**Problem:** Add a property `year` to `Car.prototype` and check it on an existing instance.
**Solution:**
```
Car.prototype.year = 2021;
console.log(myCar.year); // 2021
```
**Explanation:**
Adding a property to the prototype makes it accessible to existing instances.

## 9. Verifying `instanceof`

**Problem:** Create a `Bike` constructor, make an instance, and verify `instanceof` works as expected.
**Solution:**
```
function Bike(model) {
   this.model = model;
}
const bike1 = new Bike("Mountain");
console.log(bike1 instanceof Bike); // true
```
**Explanation:**
`bike1 instanceof Bike` checks prototype chain, returns true.

## 10. Factory vs Constructor

**Problem:** Create a factory function `createDog(name)` that returns an object and compare usage with a constructor `Dog(name)`.

**Solution:**
```
function Dog(name) {
  this.name = name;
  this.bark = function() { console.log("Woof! "
+ this.name); };
}
function createDog(name) {
  return {
    name,
    bark() { console.log("Woof! " + this.name);
}
  };
}
const dog1 = new Dog("Rex");
const dog2 = createDog("Buddy");
dog1.bark(); // "Woof! Rex"
dog2.bark(); // "Woof! Buddy"
```
**Explanation:**
Dog uses new, `createDog` returns an object directly.

# Conclusion

Object constructors in JavaScript provide a powerful way to create multiple objects sharing similar structure and behavior. By leveraging prototypes and constructors (or ES6 classes), you can write more maintainable and efficient code. Understanding how new works, when to use prototypes, and how ES6 classes compare to traditional constructors is key to mastering object creation patterns in JavaScript.

# Understanding JavaScript Prototypes and Prototype Inheritance

# What Is a Prototype?

In JavaScript, every object has a hidden internal property called `[[Prototype]]` (often accessed via `Object.getPrototypeOf(obj)` or the deprecated `__proto__` accessor in some browsers). This prototype is another object from which properties and methods can be inherited. Prototypes form the foundation of JavaScript's inheritance system, which differs significantly from the classical class-based inheritance seen in languages like Java or C++.

# Key Points

1. **Prototype Link:**
When you create an object in JavaScript, it has a reference (prototype link) to another object, which is that object's prototype. This link is established at object creation time.
2. **Prototype Chain:**
If you try to access a property on an object and the object doesn't have that property, JavaScript will look up its prototype chain. It will check the object's prototype, then the prototype's prototype, and so on, until it reaches the `Object.prototype`, which is the root of almost all objects in JavaScript.
3. **Object.prototype:**
Almost every object in JavaScript ultimately inherits from `Object.prototype`, which provides fundamental methods like `hasOwnProperty()`, `toString()`, and `valueOf()`.
4. **The prototype Property on Functions:**
Every function (except arrow functions and a few built-ins) has a `prototype` property, which is itself an object. When you use a function as a constructor (i.e., invoked with new), the new object's internal `[[Prototype]]` will be set to that function's `prototype` object. This is the basis of constructor-based inheritance in pre-ES6 style JavaScript.
5. **Changing the Prototype:**
You can set an object's prototype using `Object.create()`, which allows you to create a new object with a specified prototype without the need for a constructor function.

Example: `let obj = Object.create(someProtoObject);`

6. **Prototype Methods and Properties:**
Methods are often placed on the constructor's prototype, so all instances created from that constructor share the same method definitions, reducing memory usage and providing a single place to update shared logic.

7. `Object.getPrototypeOf()` and `Object.setPrototypeOf()`:
These methods let you inspect and modify (not recommended for performance reasons) the prototype of an object. The older `__proto__` accessor is generally discouraged in modern code, but still widely supported.

8. **ES6 Classes and Prototypes:**
Although ES6 introduced the `class` syntax, under the hood it still uses prototypes. A class's methods are placed on the class's prototype, and instances created by new have their internal `[[Prototype]]` linked to that class's prototype object.

## Simple Example of Prototype Inheritance

```
function Person(name) {
  this.name = name;
}
Person.prototype.greet = function() {
  console.log("Hello, my name is " +
this.name);
};
let alice = new Person("Alice");
alice.greet(); // "Hello, my name is Alice"
// alice.__proto__ === Person.prototype
// Person.prototype.__proto__ ===
Object.prototype
```

## Using `Object.create()` to Inherit

```
let animal = {
  eat: function() {
    console.log("Eating...");
  }
};
let dog = Object.create(animal);
dog.bark = function() {
  console.log("Woof!");
};
dog.eat();  // "Eating..." (from animal)
dog.bark(); // "Woof!"
```

## Overriding Prototype Properties

If an object's own property shadows a property on its prototype,
JavaScript will use the object's own property first:

```
let proto = {
  greet: function() { console.log("Hello from
proto!"); }
};
let obj = Object.create(proto);
obj.greet(); // "Hello from proto!"
// Override greet on obj
obj.greet = function() { console.log("Hello
from obj!"); };
obj.greet(); // "Hello from obj!"
```

## Checking Own Properties vs. Inherited

```
console.log(obj.hasOwnProperty('greet')); //
true, since we defined it on obj
console.log(proto.hasOwnProperty('greet')); //
true, defined on proto
```

## Constructor vs. Prototype

```
function Person(name) {
  this.name = name;   // own property on the
instance
}
Person.prototype.introduce = function() {
  console.log("Hi, I am " + this.name);
};
let bob = new Person("Bob");
bob.introduce(); // from Person.prototype
```

# Multiple Choice Questions

**1. What is the [[Prototype]] of an object in JavaScript?**
A. A hidden property that references another object for property lookup.
B. A copy of the parent object's properties.
C. A function that returns the constructor of the object.
D. A method that defines closure.
**Answer:** A
**Explanation:** Every object has a hidden internal [[Prototype]] that points to another object from which it can inherit properties.
**2. By default, which object sits at the top of the prototype chain?**
A. Object.create()
B. Object.prototype
C. Function.prototype
D. Window.prototype
**Answer:** B
**Explanation:** At the top of the prototype chain is Object.prototype.
**3. Given function Person() {} , what does Person.prototype represent?**
A. The newly created instance of Person.
B. An object that will be the [[Prototype]] of all objects

created by new `Person()`.
C. A property that holds Person's own methods.
D. It doesn't exist by default.
**Answer:** B
**Explanation:** `Person.prototype` is the object that instances of `Person` will inherit from.
**4. What method is commonly used to create an object with a specific prototype?**
A. `Object.setPrototype()`
B. `Object.assign()`
C. `Object.create()`
D. `Object.new()`
**Answer:** C
**Explanation:** `Object.create(proto)` creates a new object with `proto` as its `[[Prototype]]`.
**5. Which property do you use to check if a property is directly defined on the object (not on its prototype)?**
A. `Object.hasOwn()`
B. `hasOwnProperty()`
C. `in` operator
D. `instanceof` operator
**Answer:** B
**Explanation:** `obj.hasOwnProperty(prop)` returns `true` if `prop` is an own property of `obj`.
**6. Consider:**
```
function Animal() {}
Animal.prototype.move = function() {
console.log("moving"); };
let cat = new Animal();
```
What happens if you call `cat.move()`?
A. Error: move is not defined on cat.
B. Logs "moving" to the console.
C. Does nothing.
D. Throws a TypeError.
**Answer:** B
**Explanation:** `cat` inherits move from `Animal.prototype`, so `cat.move()` logs "moving".

**7. How can you get the prototype of an existing object `obj`?**
A. `obj.prototype`
B. `Object.getPrototypeOf(obj)`
C. `obj.__proto__` (standard and recommended)
D. `obj.constructor`
**Answer:** B
**Explanation:** The standardized way is using `Object.getPrototypeOf(obj)`. Although `obj.__proto__` works, it's not the recommended standard approach.

**8. Which statement best describes prototype-based inheritance?**
A. Objects are linked to a chain of prototypes, and properties are looked up along this chain.
B. Classes define inheritance, and objects are instances of these classes.
C. Each object copies properties from its parent.
D. Prototypes do not exist in JavaScript.
**Answer:** A
**Explanation:** JavaScript uses prototype-based inheritance where objects inherit properties from their prototypes dynamically.

**9. If `obj` is created by `let obj = Object.create(null);`, what is true about `obj`?**
A. `obj` has no prototype.
B. `obj` inherits from `Object.prototype`.
C. `obj` has a `toString()` method.
D. `obj` has a `constructor` property.
**Answer:** A
**Explanation:** `Object.create(null)` creates an object with no prototype, so it doesn't inherit any properties, not even `toString()` from `Object.prototype`.

**10. If you assign `obj.__proto__ = anotherObj;` what is the effect?**
A. `obj` will now inherit from `anotherObj`.
B. Nothing, since `__proto__` is not used in modern JavaScript.

C. `anotherObj` will be deleted.

D. `obj` and `anotherObj` become the same object.

**Answer:** A

**Explanation:** Setting `obj.__proto__` to `anotherObj` changes `obj`'s prototype chain so that it inherits from `anotherObj`. Although not recommended, it still works in many JavaScript environments.

**11. What is the prototype chain of `let arr = [1,2,3];` typically?**

A. arr → Object.prototype → null

B. arr → Array.prototype → Object.prototype → null

C. arr → Function.prototype → Object.prototype → null

D. arr → null

**Answer:** B

**Explanation:** Arrays inherit from `Array.prototype`, which in turn inherits from `Object.prototype`.

**12. Which built-in method can be used to verify if a property is found on the object or its prototype chain?**

A. `hasOwnProperty()`

B. `propertyIsEnumerable()`

C. The `in` operator

D. `Object.keys()`

**Answer:** C

**Explanation:** The `in` operator returns `true` if a property exists either directly on the object or somewhere in its prototype chain.

**13. In the context of prototypes, what does `constructor` property usually point to?**

A. The function that created the instance's prototype.

B. The global Object constructor.

C. Always `Object()`.

D. It's a deprecated property.

**Answer:** A

**Explanation:** By default, `Foo.prototype.constructor = Foo`. Instances created by `new Foo()` have a `constructor` property on their prototype that points back to Foo.

**14. What is the recommended modern method to set the prototype of an object after creation?**

A. `obj.__proto__ = ...`
B. `Object.setPrototypeOf(obj, newProto)`
C. `obj.prototype = newProto;`
D. `Object.create(proto)`

**Answer:** B

**Explanation:** `Object.setPrototypeOf` is the standardized way to set the prototype of an existing object, though it's slow and not generally encouraged for performance reasons. The best practice is to create objects with the desired prototype using `Object.create()` rather than modifying them later.

**15. Given:**

```
function Person() {}
Person.prototype = { sayHi: function() {
console.log("Hi"); } };
let p = new Person();
```

What is true about p?

A. p inherits sayHi from its prototype.
B. p does not have access to sayHi because `prototype` was reassigned.
C. p is not an instance of Person anymore.
D. p has sayHi as its own property.

**Answer:** A

**Explanation:** By reassigning `Person.prototype`, we set a new prototype object. Now instances of `Person` will inherit from this new object, so `p.sayHi()` works.

**16. Which one is NOT a recommended way to access the prototype of an object?**

A. `Object.getPrototypeOf(obj)`
B. `obj.__proto__`
C. `obj.constructor.prototype`
D. `obj.prototype`

**Answer:** D

**Explanation:** `obj.prototype` is not correct because `prototype` is a property on functions, not on arbitrary objects.

`obj.__proto__` and `Object.getPrototypeOf(obj)` are common ways, although `obj.__proto__` is not recommended. `obj.constructor.prototype` works if `constructor` is reliable.

**17. If child is created with `Object.create(parent)`, what is `Object.getPrototypeOf(child) === parent`?**
A. True
B. False
**Answer:** A
**Explanation:** `Object.create(parent)` creates a new object with `parent` as its prototype.

**18. If you redefine `Parent.prototype` entirely after creating some instances, do the existing instances see the changes?**
A. Yes, immediately.
B. No, they keep referencing the old prototype object.
C. Only if you run a special method.
D. They lose all their methods.
**Answer:** B
**Explanation:** Existing instances reference the old prototype object they were created with. Changing the `Parent.prototype` to a new object affects only newly created objects.

**19. What does `instanceof` operator check?**
A. If an object directly contains a property.
B. If the object inherits from the constructor's prototype chain.
C. If a property exists in the prototype.
D. If two objects are identical.
**Answer:** B
**Explanation:** `obj instanceof Constructor` checks if `obj`'s prototype chain includes `Constructor.prototype`.

**20. Which method returns a boolean indicating whether the given object is in the prototype chain of another object?**
A. `isPrototypeOf()`
B. `hasOwnProperty()`
C. `propertyIsEnumerable()`
D. `Object.prototypeIn()`

**Answer:** A
**Explanation:** `prototypeObj.isPrototypeOf(obj)` returns
`true` if `prototypeObj` is in `obj`'s prototype chain.

# 10 Coding Exercises with Solutions and Explanations

**Exercise 1:**
Create a constructor function `Car` that sets a `model` property
from a parameter, and add a method `drive()` to
`Car.prototype`. Then create an instance and call the method.
**Solution:**
```
function Car(model) {
   this.model = model;
}
Car.prototype.drive = function() {
   console.log("Driving a " + this.model);
};
let tesla = new Car("Tesla Model 3");
tesla.drive(); // "Driving a Tesla Model 3"
```
**Explanation:** We define a constructor and assign a method to
its prototype. Instances inherit the `drive()` method.
**Exercise 2:**
Use `Object.create()` to create an object `student` that
inherits from `person` and overrides a property.
**Solution:**
```
let person = {
   species: "Homo sapiens",
   greet: function() { console.log("Hello!"); }
};
let student = Object.create(person);
student.major = "Computer Science";
student.greet(); // "Hello!"
console.log(student.species); // "Homo sapiens"
```

**Explanation:** student inherits from person. It gains greet and species, and also has its own major property.

**Exercise 3:**

Create an object rectangle with width and height, and add a method area() on its prototype using Object.create(). Then create a square object that inherits from rectangle and set width and height to the same value.

**Solution:**

```
let rectangle = {
    width: 0,
    height: 0,
    area: function() {
        return this.width * this.height;
    }
};
let square = Object.create(rectangle);
square.width = 5;
square.height = 5;
console.log(square.area()); // 25
```

**Explanation:** square inherits the area() method from rectangle.

**Exercise 4:**

Create a function Animal(name) and add a method speak() to its prototype. Then create a Dog constructor that inherits from Animal and overrides the speak() method.

**Solution:**

```
function Animal(name) {
    this.name = name;
}
Animal.prototype.speak = function() {
    console.log(this.name + " makes a noise.");
};
function Dog(name) {
    Animal.call(this, name);
}
// Inherit from Animal
```

```
Dog.prototype =
Object.create(Animal.prototype);
Dog.prototype.constructor = Dog;
Dog.prototype.speak = function() {
  console.log(this.name + " barks.");
};
let rufus = new Dog("Rufus");
rufus.speak(); // "Rufus barks."
```
**Explanation:** We create an inheritance chain by setting
`Dog.prototype = Object.create(Animal.prototype)`.
We then override `speak()`.

**Exercise 5:**
Check if `Object.prototype` is in the prototype chain of an array `[1,2,3]` using `isPrototypeOf()`.
**Solution:**
```
let arr = [1,2,3];
console.log(Object.prototype.isPrototypeOf(arr)
); // true
```
**Explanation:** Arrays inherit from `Array.prototype`, and `Array.prototype` inherits from `Object.prototype`.

**Exercise 6:**
Create an object without a prototype using `Object.create(null)`, and show that `toString()` is not available.
**Solution:**
```
let objWithoutProto = Object.create(null);
console.log(objWithoutProto.toString); //
undefined
```
**Explanation:** Since the object has no prototype, it doesn't inherit `toString()` from `Object.prototype`.

**Exercise 7:**
Given a constructor `Person`, add a static method to it by attaching a function to `Person` directly (not on its prototype). Show that instances do not have this method.
**Solution:**

```
```

```
function Person(name) {
  this.name = name;
}
Person.prototype.sayName = function() {
  console.log("My name is " + this.name);
};
Person.describe = function() {
  console.log("This is a Person constructor.");
};
let bob = new Person("Bob");
bob.sayName();        // "My name is Bob"
console.log(bob.describe); // undefined - it's
not inherited
Person.describe();    // "This is a Person
constructor."
```
**Explanation:** Static methods are attached to the constructor function itself, not the prototype, so instances don't inherit them.

**Exercise 8:**
Use Object.getPrototypeOf() to confirm the prototype of a newly created object.

**Solution:**
```
let baseObj = { hello: "world" };
let derivedObj = Object.create(baseObj);
console.log(Object.getPrototypeOf(derivedObj)
=== baseObj); // true
```
**Explanation:** Object.getPrototypeOf() returns baseObj, confirming the inheritance relationship.

**Exercise 9:**
Create a chain of three objects: grandparent, parent, and child, using Object.create(). Have child access a property defined in grandparent.

**Solution:**
```
let grandparent = { familyName: "Smith" };
let parent = Object.create(grandparent);
let child = Object.create(parent);
console.log(child.familyName); // "Smith"
```

**Explanation:** The property lookup goes `child -> parent ->` `grandparent`, and finds `familyName` at `grandparent`.
**Exercise 10:**
Demonstrate that changing a prototype property affects all instances that inherit from it, unless they have overridden that property.
**Solution:**
```
function Person(name) {
  this.name = name;
}
Person.prototype.greet = function() {
  console.log("Hello, I'm " + this.name);
};
let alice = new Person("Alice");
let tom = new Person("Tom");
alice.greet(); // "Hello, I'm Alice"
tom.greet();   // "Hello, I'm Tom"
Person.prototype.greet = function() {
  console.log("Hi, I'm " + this.name);
};
alice.greet(); // "Hi, I'm Alice"
tom.greet();   // "Hi, I'm Tom"
// Override greet on alice
alice.greet = function() {
  console.log("Alice says hi differently.");
};
alice.greet(); // "Alice says hi differently."
tom.greet();   // still "Hi, I'm Tom"
```
**Explanation:** Changing `Person.prototype.greet` affects all instances because they inherit the updated function. However, once `alice` overrides `greet` locally, changes to the prototype no longer affect `alice`'s `greet()` method.

# Summary

- JavaScript uses prototype-based inheritance: each object inherits properties and methods from its prototype.
- The prototype chain is traversed when looking up properties.
- Constructors, `Object.create()`, and `Object.getPrototypeOf()` help manage and understand prototypes.
- ES6 classes are syntactic sugar over prototypes.
- Prototype inheritance provides a dynamic and flexible system different from classical class-based inheritance.

By understanding prototypes, you gain mastery over how JavaScript objects and inheritance truly work under the hood, enabling you to write more efficient, organized, and extensible code.

# Understanding ES6 Classes in JavaScript

## Introduction to Classes

Before ES6 (ECMAScript 2015), JavaScript primarily used constructor functions and prototypes for object creation and inheritance. ES6 introduced classes as syntactical sugar on top of the existing prototype-based inheritance model. Although classes look more like classes in languages such as Java or C++, they still rely on prototypes under the hood.

## Defining a Class

A class in JavaScript is defined using the `class` keyword. Unlike function declarations, class declarations are not hoisted. You must define a class before you can instantiate it.

**Syntax:**
```
class ClassName {
    // class body
}
```

## The Constructor Method

When you create a class, you can define a special method
called `constructor()`. The constructor is automatically called
when you create a new instance of a class using new. It's
typically used to initialize instance properties.
**Example:**

```
class Person {
  constructor(name, age) {
    this.name = name;
    this.age = age;
  }
  greet() {
    console.log(`Hello! My name is ${this.name}
and I am ${this.age} years old.`);
  }
}
let alice = new Person('Alice', 30);
alice.greet(); // "Hello! My name is Alice and
I am 30 years old."
```

## Methods in Classes

Methods inside classes are defined without the `function`
keyword. They become properties of the class's prototype.
Instances share these methods, rather than each having its own
copy.
**Example:**

```
class Rectangle {
  constructor(width, height) {
    this.width = width;
    this.height = height;
  }
  area() {
    return this.width * this.height;
```

```
  }
}
let rect = new Rectangle(5, 10);
console.log(rect.area()); // 50
```

## Static Methods and Properties

You can use the `static` keyword to define methods (and properties in newer versions of JavaScript) that belong to the class itself, not to instances. Static methods are often utility functions related to the class's logic but not related to an individual instance.
**Example:**
```
class MathUtils {
  static add(a, b) {
    return a + b;
  }
}
console.log(MathUtils.add(2, 3)); // 5
// You can't call mathUtilsInstance.add(2,3) if
mathUtilsInstance is an instance
```

## Computed Method Names

You can use computed property names in class method definitions by using [ ]:
```
let methodName = 'dynamicMethod';
class Example {
  [methodName]() {
    console.log("This method name was computed
at runtime!");
  }
}
let ex = new Example();
ex.dynamicMethod(); // "This method name was
computed at runtime!"
```

## Class Expressions

Classes can also be defined using expressions (anonymous or named):

```
const PersonClass = class {
  constructor(name) {
    this.name = name;
  }
  speak() {
    console.log(`Hi, I'm ${this.name}`);
  }
};
let bob = new PersonClass('Bob');
bob.speak(); // "Hi, I'm Bob"
```

## Inheritance with extends and super

ES6 classes make inheritance more straightforward. The extends keyword sets up the prototype chain so that a derived class inherits from a base class. The derived class's constructor must call super() before using this.

**Example:**

```
class Animal {
  constructor(name) {
    this.name = name;
  }
  speak() {
    console.log(`${this.name} makes a noise.`);
  }
}
class Dog extends Animal {
  constructor(name, breed) {
    super(name); // call the parent constructor
    this.breed = breed;
  }
```

```
  speak() {
    console.log(`${this.name} barks.
${this.breed} is excited!`);
  }
}
let rufus = new Dog('Rufus', 'Labrador');
rufus.speak(); // "Rufus barks. Labrador is
excited!"
```

## Overriding Methods

Just as shown above, the derived class can define a method
with the same name as the base class method, effectively
overriding it.

## Calling Parent Methods

To call the parent's method inside a derived class's method, use
super.methodName():

```
class Parent {
  greet() {
    console.log("Hello from Parent");
  }
}
class Child extends Parent {
  greet() {
    super.greet(); // calls Parent.greet()
    console.log("Hello from Child");
  }
}
let c = new Child();
c.greet();
// "Hello from Parent"
// "Hello from Child"
```

## Important Points

- Classes are just syntactic sugar over prototypes.
- Classes cannot be called without new.
- Class declarations are not hoisted; you must define them before usage.
- The super keyword is used both for calling the parent's constructor and parent methods.
- Fields (class properties declared inside the class body) were added in later versions of JavaScript and may need certain language features or transpilation for cross-browser support.

# Multiple Choice Questions

1. **What is the primary purpose of the class keyword in JavaScript (ES6)?**
A. To introduce classical inheritance similar to Java or C++.
B. To provide a syntactical sugar over prototype-based inheritance.
C. To replace all functions.
D. To create private variables automatically.
**Answer:** B
**Explanation:** ES6 classes are syntactical sugar over JavaScript's existing prototype-based inheritance system.

2. **Which of the following is true about the constructor method in a class?**
A. It is called automatically when the class definition is read.
B. It is called when a new instance of the class is created with new.
C. It can only be defined once per class using the keyword construct.
D. It is optional and never called if omitted.
**Answer:** B
**Explanation:** The constructor is invoked each time you create a new instance with new.

3. **What happens if you do not define a constructor in a class?**
A. It fails to instantiate objects.
B. A default empty constructor is used.

C. No instances can be created from that class.
D. The class cannot extend another class.
**Answer:** B
**Explanation:** If no constructor is defined, a default constructor is used that basically returns this.

4. **How do you define a static method in a class?**
A. By prefixing the method name with class.
B. By putting the method inside the constructor.
C. By using the static keyword before the method name.
D. By defining the method outside of the class.
**Answer:** C
**Explanation:** The static keyword makes a method a class-level method, not tied to instances.

5. **What is required when a subclass defines a constructor?**
A. It must call super() before using this.
B. It must not have any methods.
C. It must not call super() at all.
D. It can only define properties after the constructor ends.
**Answer:** A
**Explanation:** In a subclass, super() must be called before this is accessed in the constructor.
**Consider:**

```
class Animal {
  constructor(name) {
    this.name = name;
  }
  speak() {
    console.log(`${this.name} makes a noise.`);
  }
}
class Dog extends Animal {
  speak() {
    console.log(`${this.name} barks.`);
  }
}
let r = new Dog('Rex');
r.speak();
```

6. What is the output?
A. "Rex makes a noise."
B. "Rex barks."
C. Error: must call super() in the Dog constructor.
D. Nothing.
**Answer:** B
**Explanation:** Dog overrides speak() and prints "Rex barks."

7. **Which statement about classes is false?**
A. Classes are not hoisted.
B. You cannot invoke a class without new.
C. Class bodies are executed in strict mode.
D. Class methods automatically bind this to the instance.
**Answer:** D
**Explanation:** Class methods do not automatically bind this. You must do so manually if needed.

8. **What does super() do inside a subclass constructor?**
A. Calls the parent class's constructor.
B. Calls a global function named super.
C. Declares a super variable.
D. Nothing special.
**Answer:** A
**Explanation:** super() invokes the parent class's constructor.

9. **Which keyword is used to create a subclass from a parent class?**
A. derive
B. subclass
C. extend
D. extends
**Answer:** D
**Explanation:** The extends keyword is used for inheritance.

10. **How do you properly call a parent method from a child method with the same name?**
A. super.methodName()
B. this.parent.methodName()
C. parentClassName.methodName()
D. this.super.methodName()
**Answer:** A

**Explanation:** Use super.methodName() inside the child class to call the parent's method.

**11. If a method is defined as static in a class, how do you call it?**

A. By creating an instance and then calling the method on that instance.

B. Directly on the class itself.

C. Using super.staticMethodName() always.

D. You cannot call static methods.

**Answer:** B

**Explanation:** Static methods are called on the class itself, e.g., MyClass.myStaticMethod().

**12. Which of the following best describes class fields (public instance fields)?**

A. They are properties defined inside the constructor.

B. They are a new addition allowing you to define instance properties at the top-level of the class body.

C. They automatically become private.

D. They must be defined outside the class.

**Answer:** B

**Explanation:** Public class fields allow defining instance properties without placing them in the constructor.

**13. Can you declare private fields in a class, and if so, how?**

A. Yes, by using private keyword before the field name.

B. Yes, by prefixing the field name with #.

C. No, ES6 classes do not support private fields.

D. Yes, by defining them inside a closure.

**Answer:** B

**Explanation:** Private fields are declared with a # prefix as per newer specifications (#myField).

**14. What happens if you try to extend a non-constructor object?**

A. The code throws a TypeError.

B. The class silently fails.

C. The child class just behaves like a regular class without parent.

D. It creates a new empty parent class.

**Answer:** A

**Explanation:** `class X extends Y` where Y is not a constructor or null will throw a TypeError.

15. **Which is a correct way to define a class expression?**
A. `let MyClass = class { constructor() {} };`
B. `class() {}`
C. `class { constructor() {}; }` as a statement by itself.
D. `function class() {}`
**Answer:** A
**Explanation:** You can define an anonymous class and assign it to a variable.

16. **Which statement is true about the `constructor` in an ES6 class?**
A. Every class must define a constructor.
B. If omitted, a default constructor is created automatically.
C. You can define multiple constructors in a single class.
D. The constructor cannot call `super()`.
**Answer:** B
**Explanation:** A default constructor `(...args) => { super(...args); }` is provided if not specified, in the case of inheritance, or an empty one if no inheritance.

17. **If you have `class A {}` and `class B extends A {}`, what is the prototype chain of an instance of B?**
A. `b → B.prototype → Object.prototype`

B. `b → B.prototype → A.prototype → Object.prototype`

C. `b → A.prototype → B.prototype → Object.prototype`

D. `b → Object.prototype`

**Answer:** B
**Explanation:** Instances of B inherit from B.prototype, which inherits from A.prototype, which inherits from Object.prototype.

18. **Which of these is not allowed inside a class?**
A. Defining methods.
B. Defining static methods.
C. Defining private fields with #.
D. Executing code outside of a method (top-level code directly inside the class body).

**Answer:** D

**Explanation:** The class body only allows method definitions, fields, and static fields. No arbitrary statements are allowed.

**19.  How do you add getters and setters in a class?**

A. By defining methods prefixed with `get` and `set` keywords.

B. By using `function get property() {}` inside the class.

C. By using `Object.defineProperty()` inside the constructor.

D. By defining a static method called `get`.

**Answer:** A

**Explanation:** You can define getters and setters using `get propertyName()` and `set propertyName(value)` syntax inside the class.

**20.  Classes in JavaScript run in which mode by default?**

A. Sloppy mode.

B. Strict mode.

C. Debug mode.

D. Strict mode only for static methods.

**Answer:** B

**Explanation:** All code inside a class body is executed in strict mode.

# 10 Coding Exercises with Full Solutions and Explanations

**Exercise 1:**

**Task:** Create a `Car` class that takes `model` and `year` in the constructor and has a `describe()` method that logs these values.

**Solution:**

```
class Car {
  constructor(model, year) {
    this.model = model;
    this.year = year;
  }
  describe() {
```

```
    console.log(`This car is a ${this.model}
from ${this.year}.`);
  }
}
const myCar = new Car('Toyota Camry', 2020);
myCar.describe(); // "This car is a Toyota
Camry from 2020."
```
**Explanation:** We defined a class with a constructor and a method. Instances inherit the describe() method.
**Exercise 2:**
**Task:** Add a static method isCar(obj) to the Car class that returns true if obj is an instance of Car, otherwise false.
**Solution:**
```
class Car {
  constructor(model) {
    this.model = model;
  }
  static isCar(obj) {
    return obj instanceof Car;
  }
}
const myCar = new Car('Honda Accord');
console.log(Car.isCar(myCar)); // true
console.log(Car.isCar({model: 'Fake Car'})); //
false
```
**Explanation:** Static methods are called on the class, not on instances.
**Exercise 3:**
**Task:** Create a base class Shape with a name property, and a derived class Circle that extends Shape. Circle should take name and radius in its constructor and have a method area() that returns Math.PI * radius^2.
**Solution:**
```
class Shape {
  constructor(name) {
```

```
    this.name = name;
  }
}
class Circle extends Shape {
  constructor(name, radius) {
    super(name);
    this.radius = radius;
  }
  area() {
    return Math.PI * this.radius * this.radius;
  }
}
const c = new Circle('MyCircle', 5);
console.log(c.area()); // 78.53981633974483
```

**Explanation:** `Circle` inherits from `Shape`, calls `super(name)` to initialize the parent part, and defines its own methods.

**Exercise 4:**

**Task:** Override a method. Create a `Parent` class with a method `greet()`, and a `Child` class that extends it and overrides `greet()` by first calling `super.greet()` and then logging another message.

**Solution:**

```
class Parent {
  greet() {
    console.log("Hello from Parent");
  }
}
class Child extends Parent {
  greet() {
    super.greet();
    console.log("Hello from Child");
  }
}
const kid = new Child();
kid.greet();
// "Hello from Parent"
```

```
//  "Hello from Child"
```
**Explanation:** `super.greet()` calls the parent class's
`greet()` method, then Child adds its own message.
**Exercise 5:**
**Task:** Use getters and setters. Create a `Person` class with a
`firstName` and `lastName`. Add a getter `fullName` that
returns the full name, and a setter `fullName` that splits a string
into first and last name.
**Solution:**
```
class Person {
  constructor(firstName, lastName) {
    this.firstName = firstName;
    this.lastName = lastName;
  }
  get fullName() {
    return `${this.firstName}
${this.lastName}`;
  }
  set fullName(name) {
    const [first, last] = name.split(' ');
    this.firstName = first;
    this.lastName = last;
  }
}
const p = new Person('Alice', 'Smith');
console.log(p.fullName); // "Alice Smith"
p.fullName = 'Mary Johnson';
console.log(p.firstName); // "Mary"
console.log(p.lastName);  // "Johnson"
```
**Explanation:** Getters and setters provide a nice syntax for
retrieving and updating internal properties.
**Exercise 6:**
**Task:** Create a class `Counter` with a static property `count =
0`. Each time you create a new instance of `Counter`, increment
`count`. Show the value of `Counter.count` after creating

several instances.

**Solution:**
```
class Counter {
  static count = 0;
  constructor() {
    Counter.count++;
  }
}
new Counter();
new Counter();
new Counter();
console.log(Counter.count); // 3
```
**Explanation:** Static class fields can store data at the class level. Each new instance increments the static count.

**Exercise 7:**

**Task:** Demonstrate private fields. Create a class BankAccount with a private field #balance. Add a method deposit(amount) and withdraw(amount) that adjust #balance if valid. Add a getBalance() method that returns the current balance.

*(Note: Private fields # may not be supported in all runtimes without transpilation. Assuming a modern environment.)*

**Solution:**
```
class BankAccount {
  #balance = 0;
  deposit(amount) {
    if (amount > 0) this.#balance += amount;
  }
  withdraw(amount) {
    if (amount > 0 && amount <= this.#balance)
{
      this.#balance -= amount;
    }
  }
  getBalance() {
    return this.#balance;
  }
```

```
}
const account = new BankAccount();
account.deposit(100);
account.withdraw(30);
console.log(account.getBalance()); // 70
// console.log(account.#balance); // Syntax
error: private field cannot be accessed outside
class
```
**Explanation:** The #balance field is private. It cannot be accessed outside the class.

**Exercise 8:**

**Task:** Class Expression: Create a class using a class expression and instantiate it.

**Solution:**
```
const AnimalClass = class {
  constructor(type) {
    this.type = type;
  }
  speak() {
    console.log(`${this.type} makes a sound.`);
  }
};
const cat = new AnimalClass('Cat');
cat.speak(); // "Cat makes a sound."
```
**Explanation:** Class expressions are just like class declarations but assigned to a variable.

**Exercise 9:**

**Task:** In a class hierarchy, call a parent method from a child. Use super.speak() in a Bird class that extends Animal, where both have a speak() method.

**Solution:**
```
class Animal {
  constructor(name) {
    this.name = name;
  }
```

```
  speak() {
    console.log(`${this.name} makes a generic
animal sound.`);
  }
}
class Bird extends Animal {
  speak() {
    super.speak();
    console.log(`${this.name} chirps.`);
  }
}
const parrot = new Bird('Polly');
parrot.speak();
// "Polly makes a generic animal sound."
// "Polly chirps."
```
**Explanation:** We override speak() in Bird and still access the parent's version via super.speak().

**Exercise 10:**

**Task:** Create a class User with a constructor that takes username. Add a method login() that prints a message. Create a subclass Admin that extends User and adds an adminLevel property. Override login() in Admin to print a more specialized message.

**Solution:**
```
class User {
  constructor(username) {
    this.username = username;
  }
  login() {
    console.log(`${this.username} is logged
in.`);
  }
}
class Admin extends User {
  constructor(username, adminLevel) {
    super(username);
```

```
      this.adminLevel = adminLevel;
    }
  login() {
    console.log(`Admin ${this.username} with
level ${this.adminLevel} is logged in.`);
    }
}
const user = new User('regularUser');
user.login(); // "regularUser is logged in."
const admin = new Admin('superAdmin', 10);
admin.login(); // "Admin superAdmin with level
10 is logged in."
```

**Explanation:** The Admin class inherits from `User` and overrides the `login()` method. The Admin constructor calls `super()` to initialize the `username` from `User`.

## Summary

ES6 classes provide a more familiar and cleaner syntax for creating and managing objects, constructors, and inheritance in JavaScript. Under the hood, classes still use prototypes and provide syntactic sugar rather than fundamentally changing how JavaScript's inheritance model works. By understanding classes, constructors, inheritance via `extends`, and the `super` keyword, you can write more organized and maintainable object-oriented JavaScript code.

# Understanding Encapsulation in JavaScript

### What Is Encapsulation?

Encapsulation is an object-oriented programming principle that involves bundling data (properties) and behaviors (methods) together and restricting direct access to some of these components. The idea is to hide internal implementation details and expose a clear and stable interface for interacting with the object.

In classical OOP languages like Java or C++, encapsulation is often achieved through access modifiers like `public`, `private`, and `protected`. JavaScript has historically lacked built-in privacy for object fields, but with newer language features, we now have various ways to achieve encapsulation.

## Encapsulation Before Modern Class Fields

Before ES6 and the introduction of private fields, JavaScript developers used closures and naming conventions to simulate encapsulation:

1. **Naming Conventions:**
Prefixing "private" properties with an underscore (e.g., `_secret`) to signal they are intended for internal use.

2. **Closures and the Module Pattern:**
Wrapping variables and functions in IIFEs (Immediately Invoked Function Expressions) or module patterns to prevent external access to internal variables.

**Example using closures:**

```
function createCounter() {
  let count = 0; // private variable (only
accessible inside this function)
    return {
      increment() {
        count++;
      },
      getValue() {
        return count;
      }
    };
}
const counter = createCounter();
```

```
counter.increment();
console.log(counter.getValue()); // 1
// We cannot directly access 'count' from
outside.
```

## ES6 Classes and Encapsulation

ES6 class syntax introduced a more familiar object-oriented style, but still didn't provide true privacy for instance fields. Class methods and properties defined without special syntax are public by default.

```
class Person {
  constructor(name) {
    this.name = name; // public property
  }
  greet() {
    console.log(`Hello, my name is
${this.name}`);
  }
}
```

In this example, name is public and can be accessed and changed from outside:

```
const p = new Person("Alice");
p.name = "Bob"; // allowed
p.greet(); // "Hello, my name is Bob"
```

## Private Class Fields (ES2022+)

Modern JavaScript introduced private class fields and methods using a # prefix. Private fields can only be accessed within the class body. They are truly private at runtime and cannot be accessed or modified outside the class.

**Example:**

```
class BankAccount {
  #balance; // private field
```

```javascript
  constructor(initialBalance) {
    this.#balance = initialBalance;
  }
  deposit(amount) {
    if (amount > 0) {
      this.#balance += amount;
    }
  }
  withdraw(amount) {
    if (amount > 0 && amount <= this.#balance)
{
      this.#balance -= amount;
    }
  }
  getBalance() {
    return this.#balance;
  }
}
const account = new BankAccount(100);
account.deposit(50);
console.log(account.getBalance()); // 150
// console.log(account.#balance); //
```
SyntaxError: Private field '#balance' must be declared in an enclosing class

**Key Points About Private Fields:**

- Declared with a # prefix.
- Must be declared before use inside the class body.
- Inaccessible outside of the class's methods.
- Even subclasses cannot access their parent's private fields directly.

## Public vs Private Fields

- **Public fields**: Declared without #, can be accessed and modified outside the class.

- **Private fields**: Declared with #, accessible only within the class's methods or getters/setters. Not accessible outside or through this from outside code.

## Static Members

**Static members** are properties and methods that belong to the class itself, rather than instances of the class. You define them with the static keyword. They are often used as utility functions or constants relevant to the class but not tied to individual instances.
**Example:**
```
class MathUtils {
  static PI = 3.14159;
  static add(a, b) {
    return a + b;
  }
}
console.log(MathUtils.PI);       // 3.14159
console.log(MathUtils.add(2, 3)); // 5
// Cannot do: const m = new MathUtils(); m.PI
is not instance-bound
```
Static fields and methods cannot access instance properties directly since they don't operate on instances, and this inside a static method refers to the class, not an instance.

## Combining Access Modifiers

While JavaScript does not have traditional public/private keywords (other than the # for private fields), you can achieve a mixture of public and private members using:
- Public instance fields and methods (no #).
- Private instance fields and methods (# fields).
- Static fields and methods (with static keyword).
This combination allows you to define a clear API (public interface) and hide internal details (private fields).

**Example:**
```javascript
class Employee {
  #salary; // private
  static company = "ABC Corp"; // static public
field
  constructor(name, salary) {
    this.name = name; // public
    this.#salary = salary; // private
  }
  // public method
  getInfo() {
    console.log(`Name: ${this.name}, Salary:
${this.#salary}`);
  }
  // private method (ES2022+)
  #calculateBonus() {
    return this.#salary * 0.1;
  }
  giveBonus() {
    const bonus = this.#calculateBonus();
    this.#salary += bonus;
  }
}
const emp = new Employee("John", 1000);
emp.getInfo(); // "Name: John, Salary: 1000"
emp.giveBonus();
emp.getInfo(); // "Name: John, Salary: 1100"
// emp.#salary = 2000; // Error: Cannot access
private field
// emp.#calculateBonus(); // Error: Cannot
access private method
console.log(Employee.company); // "ABC Corp"
```

# Multiple Choice Questions

1. **What is encapsulation in JavaScript?**
A. Bundling data and methods together and hiding internal details.
B. Writing all code in one line.
C. Having only global variables.
D. Using only arrow functions.
**Answer:** A
**Explanation:** Encapsulation hides internal complexity and provides a clear interface.

2. **How were private members commonly simulated in JavaScript before private fields existed?**
A. Using `private` keyword.
B. Using closures and naming conventions (e.g., underscores).
C. By declaring variables with `var`.
D. By using the `protected` keyword.
**Answer:** B
**Explanation:** Prior to private fields, closures and naming conventions like _privateVar were common patterns.

3. **Which of the following syntax declares a private field in a class?**
A. `private myField = 0;`
B. `_myField = 0;`
C. `#myField = 0;`
D. `this.myField = 0;`
**Answer:** C
**Explanation:** Private class fields start with #.

4. **What happens if you try to access a private field outside of the class?**
A. Returns `undefined`.
B. Throws a SyntaxError or ReferenceError.
C. Automatically becomes a public field.
D. Logs a warning in the console.
**Answer:** B
**Explanation:** Accessing a private field outside the class body is not allowed and results in an error.

5. **Static methods and properties:**
A. Are available only on class instances.

B. Are defined using the `static` keyword and exist on the class itself.
C. Cannot use the `this` keyword.
D. Must always return a value.
**Answer:** B
**Explanation:** Static methods and properties are called on the class directly, not on instances.

6. **Can a subclass access its parent's private fields directly?**
A. Yes, if it uses `super`.
B. Yes, if they are static.
C. No, private fields are not accessible by subclasses.
D. Only if the fields are marked as `protected`.
**Answer:** C
**Explanation:** Private fields are not accessible by subclasses.

7. **Which of these best describes the purpose of encapsulation?**
A. To reduce code size.
B. To hide implementation details and protect data integrity.
C. To make all properties global.
D. To allow arbitrary changes to data.
**Answer:** B
**Explanation:** Encapsulation ensures internal details are hidden, making APIs safer and more stable.

8. **If you define a method as `static greet() {}` inside a class Person, how do you call it?**
A. `let p = new Person(); p.greet();`
B. `Person.greet()`
C. `greet()` directly
D. `new Person().static.greet()`
**Answer:** B
**Explanation:** Static methods are called on the class itself, e.g. `Person.greet()`.

9. **What is the recommended modern approach to truly private instance fields in a JavaScript class?**
A. Using `#privateField` syntax.
B. Using underscores.
C. Using `var` inside the constructor.
D. Using `Object.seal()`.
**Answer:** A

**Explanation:** The # syntax is the standard for true private fields in modern JavaScript.

10.  **Which is NOT a characteristic of private fields in JS classes?**

A. They cannot be accessed outside the class body.

B. They start with a # symbol.

C. They can be accessed via `this.#field` inside class methods.

D. They can be dynamically added at runtime from outside.

**Answer:** D

**Explanation:** Private fields must be declared in the class body. They cannot be dynamically added or accessed externally.

11.  **If `this.#balance` is a private field in a class, how must it be declared?**

A. `this.#balance = 0;` inside the constructor without prior declaration.

B. `#balance = 0;` at the top level of the class.

C. `private balance = 0;` at the top of the class.

D. `let #balance = 0;` inside a method.

**Answer:** B

**Explanation:** Private fields must be declared at the top level of the class, e.g. `class X { #balance = 0; constructor() {} }`.

12.  **Static fields are initialized:**

A. When the first instance of the class is created.

B. As soon as the class is evaluated.

C. Only after calling a static method.

D. Never automatically.

**Answer:** B

**Explanation:** Static fields are initialized when the class itself is evaluated.

13.  **Can static methods access instance fields directly?**

A. Yes, using `this.fieldName`.

B. Yes, but only after creating an instance.

C. No, static methods have no direct access to instance fields.

D. Yes, if the field is public.

**Answer:** C

**Explanation:** Static methods are part of the class, not an instance, so they cannot directly access instance properties.

14.  **What is the advantage of using private fields over naming conventions (like _field)?**
A. Private fields are enforced by the language and truly inaccessible outside the class.
B. _field is completely private.
C. There is no difference.
D. _field can never be changed.
**Answer:** A
**Explanation:** _field is only a convention, not enforced. #field is enforced by the language.

15.  **Encapsulation helps with:**
A. Making code unreadable.
B. Ensuring that changes to internal logic don't break external code relying on the class interface.
C. Forcing global access to variables.
D. Preventing objects from being instantiated.
**Answer:** B
**Explanation:** Encapsulation creates a stable interface, so internal changes won't break external code.

16.  **Private class methods can also be declared with #?**
A. Yes, #methodName() is possible.
B. No, methods cannot be private.
C. Only if you use _methodName().
D. Methods are always public.
**Answer:** A
**Explanation:** Private methods are declared similarly to fields: #methodName() { ... }.

17.  **If you have a private field #count and a getter method getCount() { return this.#count; }, can you read #count from outside the class by calling object.#count?**
A. Yes, because getter methods make it public.
B. No, you must use getCount() to read it.
C. Yes, private fields are just syntax sugar.
D. Yes, in strict mode only.
**Answer:** B
**Explanation:** Private fields remain private. You must use the public getter.

18.  **Which of the following is a correct way to declare a static private field (assuming supported)?**
A. `static #secret = 'hidden';`
B. `#static secret = 'hidden';`
C. `private static secret = 'hidden';`
D. `static.secret = 'hidden';`
**Answer:** A
**Explanation:** Static private fields use `static #fieldName`.

19.  **What is the main reason to use static members?**
A. To store per-instance data.
B. To store information or functions relevant to all instances, or utility functions.
C. To prevent inheritance.
D. To make code run faster.
**Answer:** B
**Explanation:** Static members are useful for class-level logic or constants.

20.  **Encapsulation in JS classes does not require:**
A. Private fields for privacy.
B. Public methods for interaction.
C. Static methods for utility.
D. A specific naming convention.
**Answer:** C
**Explanation:** Encapsulation doesn't necessarily require static methods. They're an optional feature.

# 10 Coding Exercises with Full Solutions and Explanations

**Exercise 1: Task:** Create a class `Counter` with a private field `#count`. Add methods `increment()` and `getValue()` to manipulate and retrieve the count.

```
class Counter {
  #count = 0;
  increment() {
    this.#count++;
```

```
  }
  getValue() {
    return this.#count;
  }
}
const c = new Counter();
c.increment();
console.log(c.getValue()); // 1
// console.log(c.#count); // Error: private
field
```

**Explanation:** #count is private. You can only interact through `increment()` and `getValue()`.

**Exercise 2: Task:** Create a Person class with a public name field and a private #age field. Add a `getAge()` method to return the age.

```
class Person {
  #age;
  constructor(name, age) {
    this.name = name;
    this.#age = age;
  }
  getAge() {
    return this.#age;
  }
}
const p = new Person("Alice", 30);
console.log(p.name);      // "Alice"
console.log(p.getAge()); // 30
// console.log(p.#age);   // Error
```

**Explanation:** Age is private, accessible only via `getAge()`.

**Exercise 3: Task:** Add a private method `#validateAmount(amount)` inside a BankAccount class and use it in `deposit()` and `withdraw()` methods.

```
class BankAccount {
  #balance = 0;
  #validateAmount(amount) {
```

```
      return typeof amount === 'number' && amount
> 0;
  }
  deposit(amount) {
    if (this.#validateAmount(amount)) {
      this.#balance += amount;
    }
  }
  withdraw(amount) {
    if (this.#validateAmount(amount) && amount
<= this.#balance) {
      this.#balance -= amount;
    }
  }
  getBalance() {
    return this.#balance;
  }
}
const acct = new BankAccount();
acct.deposit(100);
acct.withdraw(50);
console.log(acct.getBalance()); // 50
```
**Explanation:** The #validateAmount method is private and can only be used internally.

**Exercise 4: Task:** Create a class MathUtils with a static method square(n) that returns n*n. Test it without creating an instance.

```
class MathUtils {
  static square(n) {
    return n * n;
  }
}
console.log(MathUtils.square(5)); // 25
```
**Explanation:** Static method called on the class directly.

**Exercise 5: Task:** Add a static field PI = 3.14 to MathUtils and log it.

```
class MathUtils {
  static PI = 3.14;
}
console.log(MathUtils.PI); // 3.14
```

**Explanation:** Static field PI is accessed from MathUtils itself.

**Exercise 6: Task:** Create a User class with a static private field #count to track the number of users created. Increment it in the constructor and create a static method to retrieve the count.

```
class User {
  static #count = 0;
  constructor() {
    User.#count++;
  }
  static getUserCount() {
    return User.#count;
  }
}
new User();
new User();
console.log(User.getUserCount()); // 2
```

**Explanation:** #count is a static private field, updated whenever a new user is instantiated.

**Exercise 7: Task:** Create a class Rectangle with public width, height and private method #calculateArea(). Add a public area() method that uses #calculateArea() to return area.

```
class Rectangle {
  constructor(width, height) {
    this.width = width;
    this.height = height;
  }
  #calculateArea() {
    return this.width * this.height;
  }
```

```
  area() {
    return this.#calculateArea();
  }
}
const rect = new Rectangle(5, 10);
console.log(rect.area()); // 50
// console.log(rect.#calculateArea()); //
Error: private method
```
**Explanation:** #calculateArea() is private and can only be called by area() method internally.

**Exercise 8: Task:** Define a class SecureStore that holds a private #data object. Add methods setItem(key, value) and getItem(key) to manipulate data.

```
class SecureStore {
  #data = {};
  setItem(key, value) {
    this.#data[key] = value;
  }
  getItem(key) {
    return this.#data[key];
  }
}
const store = new SecureStore();
store.setItem('token', 'abc123');
console.log(store.getItem('token')); //
'abc123'
// console.log(store.#data); // Error
```
**Explanation:** #data can't be accessed outside.

**Exercise 9: Task:** Create a class Counter with a private #count and a static method resetCounter(instance) that sets the instance's count to 0 by calling a public method on the instance (like instance.reset()).

```
class Counter {
  #count = 0;
```

```
  increment() {
    this.#count++;
  }
  reset() {
    this.#count = 0;
  }
  getValue() {
    return this.#count;
  }
  static resetCounter(instance) {
    instance.reset();
  }
}
const cnt = new Counter();
cnt.increment();
cnt.increment();
console.log(cnt.getValue()); // 2
Counter.resetCounter(cnt);
console.log(cnt.getValue()); // 0
```
**Explanation:** The static method manipulates an instance by calling its public method, not by accessing private fields directly.
**Exercise 10: Task:** Combine static, private, and public features. Create a class IDGenerator with a static private field #currentID = 0. Add a static method generate() that increments #currentID and returns a new ID each time.
```
class IDGenerator {
  static #currentID = 0;
  static generate() {
    return ++this.#currentID;
  }
}
console.log(IDGenerator.generate()); // 1
console.log(IDGenerator.generate()); // 2
// console.log(IDGenerator.#currentID); //
Error: private
```

**Explanation:** `#currentID` is private and static, incremented each time `generate()` is called.

## Summary

Encapsulation in JavaScript can be achieved using private fields (#), closure-based patterns, or simply by careful design. With the modern `class` syntax, you can define private fields and methods to truly hide implementation details. Static members let you define class-level utilities and constants. Together, these features support robust, safe, and maintainable code.

# Understanding Polymorphism in JavaScript

### What Is Polymorphism?

Polymorphism is a fundamental concept in object-oriented programming that refers to the ability of a single interface or method to handle different underlying forms (data types, classes, or behavior). Essentially, it means "many forms." In simpler terms, polymorphism allows one piece of code to work with different objects in a consistent way.

### Types of Polymorphism

There are two main forms of polymorphism often discussed in OOP:

1. **Method Overriding**:
Occurs when a subclass provides a specific implementation of a method that is already defined in its superclass. The overriding method in the subclass has the same name and (usually) the same parameter list as the superclass method.

2. **Method Overloading** (Not Natively Supported in JavaScript):
Occurs when multiple methods have the same name but

different parameter lists (different signatures). The idea is that the method chosen to run depends on the arguments passed at call time.

In languages like Java or C#, method overloading is supported by the language at compile time. JavaScript, however, does not support method overloading in the same manner. Instead, JavaScript is dynamically typed and does not have function signatures in the same way. To achieve overloading-like behavior, we rely on checking arguments.length or types inside a single function body.

# Method Overriding in JavaScript

## How Method Overriding Works

Method overriding in JavaScript typically involves inheritance. When using ES6 classes:
- Define a method in a parent class.
- In a subclass, define a method with the same name.
- The subclass's method overrides the parent's implementation.

**Example Using Classes:**

```
class Animal {
  speak() {
    console.log("The animal makes a sound.");
  }
}
class Dog extends Animal {
  speak() {
    console.log("The dog barks.");
  }
}
const animal = new Animal();
animal.speak(); // "The animal makes a sound."
const dog = new Dog();
dog.speak(); // "The dog barks."
```

Here, Dog overrides the speak() method from Animal. This is polymorphism: the speak() method acts differently depending on the object's type.

# Method Overloading in JavaScript

## Why JavaScript Doesn't Natively Support Overloading

In strongly typed languages, the compiler can distinguish methods by their parameter types and counts. JavaScript, being dynamically typed, does not create distinct method signatures based on parameter count or type. If you define two methods with the same name in a class, the latter definition overwrites the former.

## Simulating Method Overloading

To simulate overloading, you can write a single method that checks the number or types of arguments and performs different actions:

**Example:**

```
function greet() {
  if (arguments.length === 0) {
    console.log("Hello!");
  } else if (arguments.length === 1) {
    console.log("Hello, " + arguments[0] +
"!");
  } else {
    console.log("Hello everyone!");
  }
}
greet();            // "Hello!"
greet("Alice");     // "Hello, Alice!"
greet("Alice", "Bob"); // "Hello everyone!"
```

You could also use rest parameters and type checks:

```
function add(...args) {
  if (args.length === 1) {
    return args[0] + 10;
  } else if (args.length === 2) {
    return args[0] + args[1];
  } else {
    return args.reduce((sum, num) => sum + num,
0);
  }
}
console.log(add(5));        // 15 (treat single
arg differently)
console.log(add(2,3));      // 5    (two args
add)
console.log(add(1,2,3,4)); // 10   (multiple
args sum)
```

## Overloading Methods in Classes

You can apply a similar logic in class methods by having one method do multiple jobs based on arguments:

```
class Calculator {
  calculate(...args) {
    if (args.length === 1) {
      return args[0] * 2;
    } else if (args.length === 2) {
      return args[0] + args[1];
    } else {
      return args.reduce((a, b) => a + b, 0);
    }
  }
}
const calc = new Calculator();
console.log(calc.calculate(5));      // 10
console.log(calc.calculate(2,3));    // 5
```

```
console.log(calc.calculate(1,2,3,4)); // 10
```

# Multiple Choice Questions

1. **What is polymorphism?**
A. Ability for a function to return multiple values.
B. Ability for a single interface to represent multiple underlying forms.
C. JavaScript's use of first-class functions.
D. Storing multiple objects in a single variable.
**Answer:** B
**Explanation:** Polymorphism allows one interface (like a method name) to be used for different underlying types or behaviors.
2. **Which form of polymorphism does JavaScript naturally support through inheritance?**
A. Method overloading
B. Method overriding
C. Operator overloading
D. Constructor overloading
**Answer:** B
**Explanation:** JavaScript supports method overriding via prototype and class inheritance. Method overloading is not natively supported.
3. **What is method overriding?**
A. Defining two methods with the same name but different parameters.
B. Providing a new implementation of a method in a subclass that exists in the parent class.
C. Using arrow functions in classes.
D. Calling a function multiple times.
**Answer:** B
**Explanation:** Method overriding happens when a subclass redefines a method inherited from its superclass.
4. **Which language feature is used to implement method overriding in JavaScript (ES6)?**
A. Classes and the `extends` keyword
B. The `overload` keyword
C. The `superclass` keyword

81

D. The `methodOverride()` function

**Answer:** A

**Explanation:** Classes and the `extends` keyword create subclass relationships allowing overriding.

**5. Is method overloading directly supported by JavaScript classes?**

A. Yes, by defining multiple constructors.

B. Yes, by using parameter type annotations.

C. No, but it can be simulated with argument checks.

D. Yes, if you enable strict mode.

**Answer:** C

**Explanation:** JavaScript does not have traditional method overloading. We must check arguments inside a single method.

**6. In polymorphism, what determines which method implementation is executed at runtime when overriding?**

A. The name of the variable.

B. The type (class) of the object at runtime.

C. The number of arguments passed.

D. The line number in the code.

**Answer:** B

**Explanation:** With overriding, which method runs depends on the actual type of the object at runtime.

**Given:**

```
class Vehicle {
   move() { console.log("Vehicle moves"); }
}
class Car extends Vehicle {
   move() { console.log("Car drives"); }
}
let v = new Car();
v.move();
```

**7. What is the output?**

A. "Vehicle moves"

B. "Car drives"

C. Error: method overriding not allowed

D. Undefined

**Answer:** B

**Explanation:** Car overrides move() and v is a Car instance, so "Car drives" logs.

**8. Method overloading in JavaScript can be emulated by:**

A. Using different function names.

B. Checking arguments.length or the types of arguments inside one function.

C. Declaring methods with overload keyword.

D. Using Object.create() method.

**Answer:** B

**Explanation:** Overloading must be manually simulated by inspecting arguments at runtime.

**9. Which of the following best describes method overloading in strongly typed languages (like Java)?**

A. Defining multiple methods with the same name but different parameter signatures.

B. Defining multiple classes with the same name.

C. Using arrow functions instead of normal functions.

D. Is not possible in Java.

**Answer:** A

**Explanation:** Method overloading in strongly typed languages is about different parameter lists.

**10. In JavaScript, what happens if you define two methods with the same name in a class?**

A. Both methods are available as overloaded methods.

B. The second method definition overwrites the first.

C. The code throws a syntax error.

D. They combine their bodies.

**Answer:** B

**Explanation:** Later definitions overwrite earlier ones with the same name.

**11. Which keyword is used to call the parent class method when overriding in a subclass?**

A. parent

B. super

C. base

D. this

**Answer:** B

**Explanation:** super is used to call parent class methods in a subclass.

**12. Can you achieve polymorphism without classes in JavaScript?**

A. No, classes are mandatory.

B. Yes, by using prototypes and objects.

C. Only by using arrow functions.

D. Only by using closures.

**Answer:** B

**Explanation:** Prototypal inheritance allows polymorphism even without class syntax.

**13. What is a practical use of polymorphism?**

A. Making code more complex.

B. Allowing the same function call to work differently with different object types.

C. To reduce performance.

D. To disable inheritance.

**Answer:** B

**Explanation:** Polymorphism makes code more flexible and easier to extend.

**14. If a subclass does not override a method from the parent class, calling that method on a subclass instance will:**

A. Call the parent's method.

B. Throw an error.

C. Do nothing.

D. Call a random method.

**Answer:** A

**Explanation:** If not overridden, the inherited method from the parent is used.

**15. Method overloading is commonly implemented in JavaScript by:**

A. Type-checking and argument counting in a single method.

B. Declaring function methodName() multiple times.

C. Using @overload annotations.

D. Using a special library.

**Answer:** A

**Explanation:** Checking arguments within one method is the common approach.

16. **What does `super()` do in a subclass constructor?**
A. Calls a static method.
B. Calls the parent class's constructor.
C. Calls a global function named super.
D. Creates a new object.
**Answer:** B
**Explanation:** `super()` is used to initialize the parent class before using `this`.

17. **Polymorphism allows code to:**
A. Be less reusable.
B. Depend heavily on specific class implementations.
C. Treat objects of different types uniformly.
D. Avoid inheritance entirely.
**Answer:** C
**Explanation:** Polymorphism enables treating different objects with a common interface uniformly.

18. **Is it possible to detect which overload of a method is chosen at runtime in JavaScript?**
A. There are no real overloads, so the logic must handle it at runtime.
B. Yes, the JS engine chooses based on types.
C. Yes, by `typeof method` checks.
D. Not needed, JS automatically chooses correctly.
**Answer:** A
**Explanation:** JS does not have native overloads; you implement logic inside the method to behave differently.

19. **Which approach does not help in simulating method overloading in JavaScript?**
A. Using default parameters.
B. Checking `arguments.length`.
C. Checking the type of arguments.
D. Using separate methods with distinct names.
**Answer:** D
**Explanation:** Using separate method names is not overloading, it's just different methods. Overloading involves same name, different argument handling.

20. **Method overriding requires:**
A. Two methods with the same name and signature in the same

class.
B. A superclass and a subclass relationship.
C. Checking arguments.
D. The overrides keyword.
**Answer:** B
**Explanation:** Overriding happens in an inheritance scenario (superclass and subclass).

# 10 Coding Exercises with Solutions and Explanations

**Exercise 1:**
**Task:** Create a base class Animal with a speak() method. Create a subclass Cat that overrides speak() and prints "Meow" instead of the base message.
**Solution:**
```
class Animal {
  speak() {
    console.log("The animal speaks.");
  }
}
class Cat extends Animal {
  speak() {
    console.log("Meow");
  }
}
const genericAnimal = new Animal();
genericAnimal.speak(); // "The animal speaks."
const kitty = new Cat();
kitty.speak(); // "Meow"
```
**Explanation:** Cat overrides the speak() method from Animal.
**Exercise 2:**
**Task:** Using a single function displayInfo(), handle different numbers of arguments:
• No arguments: print "No info".
• One argument: print "Info: [arg]".
• Two arguments: print "Detailed info: [arg1], [arg2]".

**Solution:**
```
function displayInfo() {
  if (arguments.length === 0) {
    console.log("No info");
  } else if (arguments.length === 1) {
    console.log("Info: " + arguments[0]);
  } else if (arguments.length === 2) {
    console.log("Detailed info: " +
arguments[0] + ", " + arguments[1]);
  }
}
displayInfo();              // "No info"
displayInfo("Data");        // "Info: Data"
displayInfo("Data", 123); // "Detailed info:
Data, 123"
```
**Explanation:** This simulates overloading by checking
`arguments.length`.

**Exercise 3:**

**Task:** Create a Shape class with a `draw()` method. Create
`Circle` and `Square` classes that extend Shape and override
`draw()`. Call `draw()` on instances of both subclasses.

**Solution:**
```
class Shape {
  draw() {
    console.log("Drawing a generic shape.");
  }
}
class Circle extends Shape {
  draw() {
    console.log("Drawing a circle.");
  }
}
class Square extends Shape {
  draw() {
    console.log("Drawing a square.");
```

```
    }
}
const c = new Circle();
c.draw(); // "Drawing a circle."
const s = new Square();
s.draw(); // "Drawing a square."
```
**Explanation:** Each subclass provides its own version of
`draw()`.
**Exercise 4:**
**Task:** In a single `calculate()` function, if called with one
number, return its double, if with two numbers, return their
product, else sum all arguments.
**Solution:**
```
function calculate(...args) {
  if (args.length === 1) {
    return args[0] * 2;
  } else if (args.length === 2) {
    return args[0] * args[1];
  } else {
    return args.reduce((sum, val) => sum + val,
0);
  }
}
console.log(calculate(10));      // 20
console.log(calculate(2, 3));    // 6
console.log(calculate(1,2,3,4)) // 10
```
**Explanation:** Polymorphic behavior based on argument count.
**Exercise 5:**
**Task:** Create a `Logger` class with a `log()` method. Override
`log()` in a subclass `FileLogger` that prints "Logging to file: ..."
instead of the base log message.
**Solution:**
```
class Logger {
  log(message) {
    console.log("Default logger: " + message);
  }
}
```

```javascript
class FileLogger extends Logger {
  log(message) {
    console.log("Logging to file: " + message);
  }
}
const logger = new Logger();
logger.log("Hello"); // "Default logger: Hello"
const fileLogger = new FileLogger();
fileLogger.log("Hello"); // "Logging to file:
Hello"
```

**Explanation:** FileLogger overrides `log()`.

**Exercise 6:**

**Task:** Create a function `formatDate()` that:
- If given one argument (Date object), returns a string in "YYYY-MM-DD" format.
- If given two arguments (day, month), returns a string "DD/MM".
- Otherwise, returns "Invalid Format".

**Solution:**

```javascript
function formatDate(...args) {
  if (args.length === 1 && args[0] instanceof
Date) {
    const d = args[0];
    return `${d.getFullYear()}-
${String(d.getMonth()+1).padStart(2,'0')}-
${String(d.getDate()).padStart(2,'0')}`;
  } else if (args.length === 2 && typeof
args[0] === 'number' && typeof args[1] ===
'number') {
    return
`${String(args[0]).padStart(2,'0')}/${String(ar
gs[1]).padStart(2,'0')}`;
  } else {
    return "Invalid Format";
  }
```

```
}
console.log(formatDate(new Date(2020, 0, 5)));
// "2020-01-05"
console.log(formatDate(5, 1)); // "05/01"
console.log(formatDate()); // "Invalid Format"
```
**Explanation:** This is a contrived example to show argument-based logic.

**Exercise 7:**

**Task:** Create a base class `Player` with method `play()`. A subclass `VideoPlayer` overrides `play()` to print "Playing video" and `AudioPlayer` overrides `play()` to print "Playing audio".

**Solution:**
```
class Player {
  play() {
    console.log("Playing media.");
  }
}
class VideoPlayer extends Player {
  play() {
    console.log("Playing video.");
  }
}
class AudioPlayer extends Player {
  play() {
    console.log("Playing audio.");
  }
}
const v = new VideoPlayer();
v.play(); // "Playing video."
const a = new AudioPlayer();
a.play(); // "Playing audio."
```
**Explanation:** Method overriding for polymorphic behavior.

**Exercise 8:**

**Task:** Implement a function `processData()` that:
- If given a single string, returns it uppercased.
- If given two strings, returns them concatenated.

- Otherwise, returns null.

**Solution:**

```
function processData(...args) {
  if (args.length === 1 && typeof args[0] ===
'string') {
    return args[0].toUpperCase();
  } else if (args.length === 2 && typeof
args[0] === 'string' && typeof args[1] ===
'string') {
    return args[0] + args[1];
  } else {
    return null;
  }
}
console.log(processData("hello"));        //
"HELLO"
console.log(processData("hello", "world")); //
"helloworld"
console.log(processData()); // null
```

**Explanation:** Emulated overloading via argument checks.

**Exercise 9**:

**Task:** Create a class BasePrinter with a print() method. Create a subclass ColorPrinter that overrides print() to add "in color:" before the message.

**Solution:**

```
class BasePrinter {
  print(message) {
    console.log("Printing: " + message);
  }
}
class ColorPrinter extends BasePrinter {
  print(message) {
    console.log("Printing in color: " +
message);
  }
```

```
}
const bp = new BasePrinter();
bp.print("Test"); // "Printing: Test"
const cp = new ColorPrinter();
cp.print("Test"); // "Printing in color: Test"
```
**Explanation:** Simple overriding example.

**Exercise 10:**

**Task:** Write a mathOperation() function that:

- With one number n, returns n*n.
- With two numbers (a,b), returns a + b.
- With more than two, returns their sum.

**Solution:**

```
function mathOperation(...args) {
  if (args.length === 1) {
    return args[0] * args[0];
  } else if (args.length === 2) {
    return args[0] + args[1];
  } else {
    return args.reduce((sum, val) => sum + val,
0);
  }
}
console.log(mathOperation(5));        // 25
console.log(mathOperation(2,3));      // 5
console.log(mathOperation(1,2,3,4));  // 10
```
**Explanation:** Another example of simulated overloading.

# Summary

Polymorphism in JavaScript is achieved primarily through method overriding—subclasses providing specialized implementations of methods defined in their superclasses. True method overloading (as seen in statically typed languages) is not natively supported. Instead, developers simulate overloading by inspecting the arguments within a single function or method body and altering the behavior based on argument count and types.

Polymorphism increases code flexibility, making it easier to write generic code that can work with different objects that share a common interface but have distinct implementations.
By understanding and applying these concepts, you can write more maintainable, scalable, and clean object-oriented code in JavaScript.

# Understanding Inheritance in JavaScript

## What is Inheritance?

Inheritance is a fundamental concept in object-oriented programming. It allows one class (a subclass or child class) to acquire the properties and methods of another class (a superclass or parent class). By doing so, subclasses can reuse and build upon the existing functionality, reducing code duplication and improving maintainability.

## Inheritance in JavaScript (ES6 Classes)

Prior to ES6, inheritance in JavaScript was handled through prototypes and constructor functions. ES6 introduced the class syntax, which provides a more familiar, class-based approach to inheritance, although under the hood it is still prototype-based.
**Key Keywords for Inheritance:**
- extends: Used in a class declaration or class expression to create a subclass.
- super: Used to call the parent class's constructor or parent methods.

## The extends Keyword

When you write class Child extends Parent, you are creating a subclass Child that inherits all the methods and properties of the `Parent` class. The `Child` class's prototype is linked to `Parent.prototype`, enabling instances of `Child` to have access to `Parent`'s instance methods.

**Example:**

```
class Animal {
    eat() {
        console.log("The animal is eating.");
    }
}
class Dog extends Animal {
    bark() {
        console.log("Woof!");
    }
}
const d = new Dog();
d.eat(); // "The animal is eating."
d.bark(); // "Woof!"
```

## The super Keyword

`super` serves two purposes in subclassing:

**1. Calling the Superclass Constructor:**
In a subclass constructor, before you can use `this`, you must call `super()` to ensure the parent's initialization logic runs. If you omit `super()`, `this` is not defined.

**2. Calling Superclass Methods:**
Inside subclass methods, you can call `super.methodName()` to invoke a method on the parent class. This allows for extending or modifying behavior rather than completely replacing it.

**Example Calling Super Constructor:**

```
class Animal {
    constructor(name) {
        this.name = name;
    }
    eat() {
        console.log(this.name + " is eating.");
```

```
    }
  }
  class Dog extends Animal {
    constructor(name, breed) {
      super(name); // calls Animal's constructor
      this.breed = breed;
    }
    bark() {
      console.log(this.name + " says woof!");
    }
  }
  const dog = new Dog("Rex", "Labrador");
  dog.eat(); // "Rex is eating."
  dog.bark(); // "Rex says woof!"
```

**Example Calling Super Method:**

```
  class Animal {
    speak() {
      console.log("The animal makes a sound.");
    }
  }
  class Cat extends Animal {
    speak() {
      super.speak(); // call parent speak
      console.log("The cat meows.");
    }
  }
  const cat = new Cat();
  cat.speak();
  // "The animal makes a sound."
  // "The cat meows."
```

## Subclassing Built-in Objects

You can also subclass built-in objects like `Array` or `Error`. This can be useful but may have subtleties depending on browser implementations.

**Example Subclassing Array:**

```
class MyArray extends Array {
  first() {
    return this[0];
  }
}
const arr = new MyArray(1, 2, 3);
console.log(arr.first()); // 1
console.log(arr instanceof MyArray); // true
console.log(arr instanceof Array);   // true
```

## Important Notes About Inheritance

- Subclasses that have a constructor must call `super()` before using `this`.
- If a subclass does not define a constructor, it gets a default one that calls `super()` with all arguments.
- The `extends` keyword sets up prototype-based inheritance under the hood.
- You can only extend from a valid constructor or `null`. Attempting to extend from a non-constructor will throw an error.

# Multiple Choice Questions

1. **What does `extends` do in a class declaration?**
A. Creates a separate class with no relation.
B. Establishes the prototype-based inheritance for the subclass from the superclass.
C. Automatically calls `super()`.
D. Copies methods from one class to another.
**Answer:** B
**Explanation:** `extends` links the subclass prototype to the superclass's prototype chain.

2. **What must a subclass constructor do before using this?**
A. Nothing special.
B. Call `this()` again.
C. Call `super()` to initialize the superclass part.
D. Assign `this` manually.
**Answer:** C
**Explanation:** The subclass constructor must call `super()` before using `this`.
3. **If a subclass does not define a constructor, what happens?**
A. You cannot instantiate the subclass.
B. It inherits the parent class's constructor automatically.
C. A default constructor is provided that calls `super(...args)`.
D. It throws a syntax error.
**Answer:** C
**Explanation:** A default constructor is generated that calls the parent constructor.
4. **`super()` in a subclass constructor:** A. Must always be called first if a constructor is defined.
B. Can be omitted if `this` is never used.
C. Calls a global function named super.
D. Is optional even if using `this`.
**Answer:** A
**Explanation:** `super()` must be called before accessing `this` in a subclass constructor.
5. **Which of the following allows calling a parent class method from a child class method?**
A. `super.parentMethod()`
B. `super.methodName()`
C. `this.super.methodName()`
D. `parent.methodName()`
**Answer:** B
**Explanation:** `super.methodName()` calls the parent's method.

6. **What happens if you try to extends from a non-constructor value?**
A. It silently fails.
B. Throws a TypeError at runtime.
C. Creates a normal object.
D. It compiles but never runs.
**Answer:** B
**Explanation:** Extending from a non-constructor results in a TypeError.

7. **In ES6 classes, how is inheritance implemented under the hood?**
A. By copying methods from parent to child.
B. By using prototype chains.
C. By compiling to Java bytecode.
D. By storing all code in a global object.
**Answer:** B
**Explanation:** Inheritance uses JavaScript's prototype mechanism under the hood.

8. **super() inside a class method (not constructor) refers to:**
A. The parent class's method with the same name.
B. The global object.
C. Always Object.prototype.
D. The child's own method.
**Answer:** A
**Explanation:** In class methods, super.methodName() calls the parent's corresponding method.

**What is a correct way to define a subclass?**

```
class Vehicle {}
// ????
```

9. A. class Car inherits Vehicle {}
B. class Car extends Vehicle {}
C. class Car super Vehicle {}
D. class Car.parent = Vehicle {}
**Answer:** B
**Explanation:** The extends keyword is the correct syntax.

10. **If class Cat extends Animal {} and you do const c = new Cat(), what is the prototype chain of c?**

A. c -> Cat.prototype -> Object.prototype
B. c -> Animal.prototype -> Cat.prototype ->
Object.prototype
C. c -> Cat.prototype -> Animal.prototype ->
Object.prototype
D. c -> Object.prototype

**Answer:** C

**Explanation:** The instance c inherits from Cat.prototype, which inherits from Animal.prototype, which inherits from Object.prototype.

11. **Can you extend built-in objects like Array?**

A. Yes, class MyArray extends Array {} is possible.
B. No, you must not extend built-ins.
C. Only if you use a special library.
D. Only in older versions of JavaScript.

**Answer:** A

**Explanation:** You can extend built-ins like Array.

12. **If a parent class has a method doWork() and the child class does not define it, what happens when you call it on an instance of the child?**

A. It calls the parent's doWork() method.
B. Error: method not found.
C. It returns undefined.
D. Throws a runtime error.

**Answer:** A

**Explanation:** Methods not overridden in the child are inherited from the parent.

13. **Which statement about super() in subclasses is true?**

A. super() must be called after this.
B. super() can only be called once.
C. super() must be called before using this in the constructor.
D. super() is optional in a subclass constructor that uses this.

**Answer:** C

**Explanation:** `super()` must be called before `this` in a subclass constructor.

**14.    If you do not define a constructor in the subclass, how are arguments passed to the parent constructor?**

A. They aren't; parent constructor is never called.

B. The subclass can't be instantiated.

C. The parent constructor is called with no arguments.

D. The arguments passed to the subclass's new call are passed automatically to `super()`.

**Answer:** D

**Explanation:** The default constructor is equivalent to `constructor(...args) { super(...args); }`.

**15.    What does `super.prop` inside a subclass method refer to?**

A. A property on the subclass instance.

B. A static property of the parent class.

C. A property on the parent class's prototype.

D. Global variable `prop`.

**Answer:** C

**Explanation:** `super.prop` accesses the parent's prototype property `prop`.

**16.    Can you extend a class that is itself extended from another class?**

A. Yes, you can chain `extends` multiple times.

B. No, only one level of inheritance is allowed.

C. You must use `super` more than once.

D. You must finalize the class first.

**Answer:** A

**Explanation:** Classes can form chains of inheritance.

**17.    If `class B extends A {}` and `class C extends B {}`, what is `Object.getPrototypeOf(C.prototype)`?**

A. A.prototype

B. B.prototype

C. Object.prototype

D. C itself

**Answer:** B

**Explanation:** `C.prototype`'s prototype is `B.prototype`.

**18.    What happens if you call `super()` more than once in a constructor?**

A. It calls the parent constructor multiple times.
B. It throws a runtime error.
C. It silently ignores extra calls.
D. It creates multiple inheritance.
**Answer:** B
**Explanation:** Calling `super()` more than once in a subclass constructor throws an error.

19. **`super()` must be called in a subclass constructor if:**
A. The subclass defines a constructor and uses `this`.
B. The subclass never uses `this`.
C. Always, even if no `this` is used.
D. Never.
**Answer:** A
**Explanation:** If you define a constructor in a subclass and use `this`, you must call `super()` first.

20. **If you want to extend a class but provide no additional methods, can you leave the subclass body empty?**
A. Yes, `class Child extends Parent {}` is valid.
B. No, you must at least have a constructor.
C. No, must have at least one method.
D. Only if using old syntax.
**Answer:** A
**Explanation:** A class body can be empty and still inherits from parent.

# 10 Coding Exercises with Full Solutions and Explanations

**Exercise 1:**
**Task:** Create a `Person` class with a constructor that takes name and a `greet()` method. Create a `Student` class that extends `Person`, adds a `grade` property, and override `greet()` to include the grade in the message.
**Solution:**
```
class Person {
  constructor(name) {
```

```
    this.name = name;
  }
  greet() {
    console.log("Hello, my name is " +
this.name);
  }
}
class Student extends Person {
  constructor(name, grade) {
    super(name);
    this.grade = grade;
  }
  greet() {
    super.greet();
    console.log("I am in grade " + this.grade);
  }
}
const s = new Student("Alice", 10);
s.greet();
// "Hello, my name is Alice"
// "I am in grade 10"
```

**Explanation:** Student calls super(name) to initialize Person's part, and overrides greet() but also calls super.greet().

**Exercise 2:**

**Task:** Create a Animal class with a sound() method that logs a generic sound. Create a Dog class that extends Animal and overrides sound() to bark. Call sound() on a Dog instance.

**Solution:**

```
class Animal {
  sound() {
    console.log("Some generic animal sound.");
  }
}
class Dog extends Animal {
  sound() {
```

```
      console.log("Woof!");
   }
}
const dog = new Dog();
dog.sound(); // "Woof!"
```
**Explanation:** Dog overrides the sound() method from Animal.
**Exercise 3:**
**Task:** Create a Vehicle class with a constructor that sets model. Create a Car class that extends Vehicle and adds a drive() method. Instantiate a Car and call drive().
**Solution:**
```
class Vehicle {
   constructor(model) {
      this.model = model;
   }
}
class Car extends Vehicle {
   drive() {
      console.log(this.model + " is driving.");
   }
}
const c = new Car("Toyota");
c.drive(); // "Toyota is driving."
```
**Explanation:** Even though Car has no constructor, it gets a default one calling super(model).
**Exercise 4:**
**Task:** Create a Shape class with a getArea() method that returns 0. Create a Rectangle class that extends Shape, has width and height, and overrides getArea() to return width * height.
**Solution:**
```
class Shape {
   getArea() {
      return 0;
   }
```

```
}
class Rectangle extends Shape {
  constructor(width, height) {
    super();
    this.width = width;
    this.height = height;
  }
  getArea() {
    return this.width * this.height;
  }
}
const rect = new Rectangle(5, 10);
console.log(rect.getArea()); // 50
```
**Explanation:** The subclass provides a meaningful getArea().
**Exercise 5:**
**Task:** Create a Logger class with a log(message) method.
Create a FileLogger that extends Logger, override log() to
prefix "File:" before the message.
**Solution:**
```
class Logger {
  log(message) {
    console.log("Log:", message);
  }
}
class FileLogger extends Logger {
  log(message) {
    console.log("File:", message);
  }
}
const fl = new FileLogger();
fl.log("Hello");
// "File: Hello"
```
**Explanation:** FileLogger changes the behavior of log().
**Exercise 6:**
**Task:** Create a User class with username. Create Admin class

104

extending User that adds `role` = `'admin'`. Print `username` and `role` from an `Admin` instance.
**Solution:**

```
class User {
  constructor(username) {
    this.username = username;
  }
}
class Admin extends User {
  constructor(username) {
    super(username);
    this.role = 'admin';
  }
}
const admin = new Admin("adminUser");
console.log(admin.username); // "adminUser"
console.log(admin.role);     // "admin"
```

**Explanation:** Admin sets an additional property after calling `super()`.

**Exercise 7:**

**Task:** Subclass the built-in `Error` class to create a custom `ValidationError`. Test by throwing a new `ValidationError("Invalid input")` and catch it.
**Solution:**

```
class ValidationError extends Error {
  constructor(message) {
    super(message);
    this.name = "ValidationError";
  }
}
try {
  throw new ValidationError("Invalid input");
} catch (e) {
  console.log(e.name);     // "ValidationError"
```

```
  console.log(e.message); // "Invalid input"
}
```
**Explanation:** Subclassing Error allows creating custom error types.
**Exercise 8:**
**Task:** Create a Product class with a getInfo() method. Create a Book class extending Product with title and author. Override getInfo() to print both title and author.
**Solution:**
```
class Product {
  getInfo() {
    return "Generic product";
  }
}
class Book extends Product {
  constructor(title, author) {
    super();
    this.title = title;
    this.author = author;
  }
  getInfo() {
    return `Book: "${this.title}" by
${this.author}`;
  }
}
const b = new Book("1984", "George Orwell");
console.log(b.getInfo()); // "Book: "1984" by
George Orwell"
```
**Explanation:** Book overrides getInfo() to provide more specific info.
**Exercise 9:**
**Task:** Create a BaseArray that extends Array and add a last() method that returns the last element. Test it with an instance.
**Solution:**
```
class BaseArray extends Array {
```

```
  last() {
    return this[this.length - 1];
  }
}
const arr = new BaseArray(1, 2, 3, 4);
console.log(arr.last()); // 4
```
**Explanation:** Subclassing Array is possible, and we add a custom method.

**Exercise 10:**

**Task:** Create a Manager class extending User (from exercise 6) that sets role = 'manager'. Log username and role.

**Solution:**

```
class User {
  constructor(username) {
    this.username = username;
  }
}
class Manager extends User {
  constructor(username) {
    super(username);
    this.role = 'manager';
  }
}
const m = new Manager("managerUser");
console.log(m.username); // "managerUser"
console.log(m.role);     // "manager"
```

**Explanation:** Similar to Admin, we create another subclass with a different role.

# Summary

Inheritance in JavaScript, facilitated by the extends keyword and the super keyword, provides a powerful way to create subclasses that build on existing classes. By calling super() in subclass constructors, you properly initialize parent class state, and by calling `super.methodName()`, you can reuse parent methods while adding or modifying behavior. With inheritance, code becomes more maintainable, reusable, and logically structured, following the principles of object-oriented programming.

# Understanding Mixins in JavaScript

## What Are Mixins?

In object-oriented programming, a **mixin** is a way to add properties and methods from one object to another, thereby mixing behaviors into multiple classes. Mixins provide a form of "multiple inheritance" since JavaScript does not natively support extending multiple classes. Instead, JavaScript uses prototype-based inheritance and typically allows a class to extend only one other class.

However, by using mixins, we can incorporate the functionality of multiple objects into a single class or instance. Mixins are often plain objects or functions that add new methods or properties to an existing class's prototype without relying on class inheritance. This helps achieve code reuse and modularity.

## Why Use Mixins?

- **Multiple Inheritance Simulation:**
Languages like Java or C++ allow multiple inheritance. JavaScript does not. Mixins fill this gap by letting you combine behaviors from multiple sources.
- **Code Reuse:**
Mixins allow you to maintain common behaviors in separate modules and apply them to different classes without duplicating code.
- **Better Organization:**
Complex behaviors can be split into smaller, more manageable units (mixins) and then reused as needed.

## Common Patterns for Mixins

**Object Mixins with `Object.assign()`**
You can directly copy properties from one object to another using `Object.assign()`. This is a simple way to add mixin behavior:

```
let canEat = {
  eat() { console.log("Eating..."); }
};
let canWalk = {
  walk() { console.log("Walking..."); }
};
class Person {
  constructor(name) {
    this.name = name;
  }
}
Object.assign(Person.prototype, canEat,
canWalk);
let john = new Person("John");
john.eat();   // "Eating..."
john.walk(); // "Walking..."
```

**Functional Mixins**
Use a function that takes a class (or constructor) and returns a new class with additional methods. This can leverage class inheritance or the prototype chain:

```
const CanEat = (BaseClass) => class extends
BaseClass {
  eat() { console.log("Eating..."); }
};
const CanWalk = (BaseClass) => class extends
BaseClass {
  walk() { console.log("Walking..."); }
};
class Person {}
```

```
class PersonWithAbilities extends
CanWalk(CanEat(Person)) {}
let alice = new PersonWithAbilities();
alice.eat();  // "Eating..."
alice.walk(); // "Walking..."
```
**Applying Mixins to Instances**
Instead of mixing into prototypes, you can apply mixins directly
to instances:

```
let canSing = {
   sing() { console.log("La la la"); }
};
let bob = {};
Object.assign(bob, canSing);
bob.sing(); // "La la la"
```
1. **Mixins vs. Composition**
Mixins are related to composition. Instead of relying purely on
class inheritance, you can compose behaviors at runtime. Mixins
are a form of composition, where multiple "behavior objects" are
combined into a single object.

## Potential Issues with Mixins

- **Name Clashes:**
If multiple mixins define the same method name, the last one
applied overwrites the previous one.
- **Code Maintenance:**
Overuse of mixins can lead to code that's hard to track since
behaviors are coming from multiple sources.
- **Lack of Strict Structure:**
Mixins are more ad-hoc than class inheritance. This flexibility is
powerful but can reduce clarity if not used carefully.

# Multiple Choice Questions

1. **What is a mixin in JavaScript?**
A. A built-in method for multiple inheritance
B. A way to combine properties and methods from multiple

```
```

sources into one object

C. A reserved keyword for class inheritance

D. A new data type for arrays

**Answer: B**

**Explanation:** Mixins are about mixing properties from different objects into one.

2. **Why are mixins used in JavaScript?**

A. To directly enable multiple class inheritance

B. To enforce private fields

C. To reuse functionality across different classes without repeating code

D. To compile TypeScript to JavaScript

**Answer: C**

**Explanation:** Mixins facilitate code reuse without native multiple inheritance.

3. **Which method can be used to apply mixin objects to a class prototype easily?**

A. `Object.apply()`

B. `Object.clone()`

C. `Object.assign()`

D. `Object.mix()`

**Answer: C**

**Explanation:** `Object.assign()` copies properties from source objects to a target object.

4. **If two mixins define a method with the same name, what happens when you mix them into a class?**

A. A compile-time error

B. The first method always wins

C. The last mixed-in method overrides the previous one

D. Both methods are merged somehow

**Answer: C**

**Explanation:** Properties defined later overwrite earlier ones.

5. **Which pattern allows you to extend a class by wrapping it in a function that returns a new class with additional methods?**

A. Prototype chaining

B. Functional mixin pattern

C. Mixin constructor pattern

D. Class patching
**Answer:** B
**Explanation:** Functional mixins use functions returning new classes that extend functionality.
6. **Mixins help simulate what aspect not natively supported by JavaScript classes?**
A. Single inheritance
B. Multiple inheritance
C. Data encapsulation
D. Strict typing
**Answer:** B
**Explanation:** Mixins simulate multiple inheritance.
7. **Are mixins part of the official ECMAScript specification as a separate language construct?**
A. Yes, introduced in ES6
B. Yes, introduced in ES2015
C. No, they are just a pattern used by developers
D. Yes, in ESNext
**Answer:** C
**Explanation:** Mixins are not language constructs, just patterns.
8. **Which is NOT a common way to implement a mixin?**
A. Using `Object.assign()` on a prototype
B. Using a function that returns a subclass
C. Using inheritance from multiple parent classes at once
D. Copying methods from one object to another
**Answer:** C
**Explanation:** Direct multiple inheritance is not supported. All other methods are common patterns.
9. **Can mixins be applied at the instance level, not just the class level?**
A. No, only on classes
B. Yes, using `Object.assign()` directly on the instance
C. Only with ES7 decorators
D. Only in strict mode
**Answer:** B
**Explanation:** Instances can also receive mixin properties directly.
10. **What is one disadvantage of using mixins excessively?**
A. They make code run faster
B. They enforce strict typing

C. They can lead to maintenance challenges due to complexity
D. They provide a well-defined structure, making code simpler
**Answer:** C
**Explanation:** Overuse can lead to complexity and harder maintenance.

**Which snippet correctly applies two mixins to a class?**

```
let canFly = { fly() { console.log("Flying"); }
};
let canSwim = { swim() {
console.log("Swimming"); } };
class Bird {}
// ????
```

11.   A. `Bird.prototype = Object.assign({}, canFly, canSwim);`
B. `Object.assign(Bird.prototype, canFly, canSwim);`
C. `Bird = canFly(canSwim(Bird));`
D. `Object.mixin(Bird, canFly, canSwim);`
**Answer:** B
**Explanation:** `Object.assign(Bird.prototype, canFly, canSwim);` merges their methods into Bird's prototype.

12.   **Functional mixins typically return:**
A. A primitive value
B. A new class that extends the given class
C. Nothing
D. A promise
**Answer:** B
**Explanation:** Functional mixins return a new class extending the given base class.

13.   **If canEat is a mixin object and Animal is a class, how to apply canEat to Animal?**
A. `Animal.mix(canEat);`
B. `Object.assign(Animal, canEat);`
C. `Object.assign(Animal.prototype, canEat);`
D. `Animal = Animal extends canEat;`

113

**Answer:** C

**Explanation:** You mix into `Animal.prototype` so that instances of `Animal` get the methods.

14. **Can mixins define constructor logic?**
A. No, they are objects and have no constructors
B. Yes, but you must call it manually
C. Yes, if they are functional and return a class extension that calls `super()`
D. Yes, always automatically

**Answer:** C

**Explanation:** Functional mixins can define and call constructors if they return class expressions.

15. **What happens if you mix in an object with getters and setters?**
A. They are ignored.
B. They are copied as ordinary properties.
C. Getters and setters are preserved if using `Object.defineProperties()` instead of `Object.assign()`.
D. Mixins cannot contain getters and setters.

**Answer:** C

**Explanation:** `Object.assign()` does not copy property descriptors fully. To preserve getters/setters, use `Object.defineProperties()`.

16. **Which principle do mixins share with composition?**
A. Inherit from one base class only
B. Build objects by combining simpler objects
C. Strict class hierarchies
D. Automatic conflict resolution

**Answer:** B

**Explanation:** Mixins and composition both emphasize building complex behavior from simpler components.

17. **Can you apply multiple functional mixins in a chain?**
A. No, only one is allowed.
B. Yes, by nesting calls like `MixinB(MixinA(BaseClass))`.
C. Only using `class ... extends ... implements ...` syntax.
D. Only in older JavaScript versions.

**Answer:** B

**Explanation:** You can chain functional mixins like `class Extended extends MixinB(MixinA(Base)) {}`.

18. **If `Bird` gets a `fly()` method from a mixin and Penguin extends `Bird` but doesn't want `fly()`, how to remove it?**

A. `delete Penguin.prototype.fly;`

B. `Penguin.mixout('fly');`

C. You cannot remove inherited methods.

D. Overwrite `fly()` with an empty function.

**Answer:** A

**Explanation:** You can delete properties from the prototype to remove them.

19. **Are mixins restricted to class-based code?**

A. Yes, only classes can use mixins.

B. No, you can use mixins with plain objects and constructors.

C. Only arrow functions can have mixins.

D. Only inside modules.

**Answer:** B

**Explanation:** Mixins work with plain objects, constructors, and classes alike.

20. **If a mixin expects certain properties to exist on the class, what concept does this resemble?**

A. Duck typing

B. Strong typing

C. Interfaces

D. Abstract classes

**Answer:** A

**Explanation:** Mixins relying on certain properties is similar to duck typing — if it quacks like a duck, treat it like a duck.

# 10 Coding Exercises with Full Solutions and Explanations

### Exercise 1:

**Task:** Create a `canTalk` mixin with a `talk()` method. Apply it to a `Person` class so that Person instances can call `talk()`.

**Solution:**

```javascript
let canTalk = {
  talk() {
    console.log("I can talk!");
  }
};
class Person {
  constructor(name) {
    this.name = name;
  }
}
Object.assign(Person.prototype, canTalk);
const p = new Person("Alice");
p.talk(); // "I can talk!"
```

**Explanation:** `Object.assign()` mixes the `talk()` method into `Person.prototype`.

**Exercise 2:**

**Task:** Define two mixins `canFly` and `canSwim`. Create a Duck class and apply both mixins so Duck can `fly()` and `swim()`.

**Solution:**

```javascript
let canFly = {
  fly() { console.log("Flying..."); }
};
let canSwim = {
  swim() { console.log("Swimming..."); }
};
class Duck {}
Object.assign(Duck.prototype, canFly, canSwim);
const d = new Duck();
d.fly();  // "Flying..."
d.swim(); // "Swimming..."
```

**Explanation:** By applying both mixins, Duck gains both behaviors.

**Exercise 3:**

**Task:** Create a functional mixin `CanSing` that takes a class and returns a new class extending it with `sing()` method. Apply it to a `Person` class.

**Solution:**

```
const CanSing = (BaseClass) => class extends
BaseClass {
   sing() {
     console.log("La la la!");
   }
};
class Person {}
class SingingPerson extends CanSing(Person) {}
const sp = new SingingPerson();
sp.sing(); // "La la la!"
```

**Explanation:** The functional mixin returns a class that extends the given `BaseClass` with new methods.

**Exercise 4:**

**Task:** You have a `Robot` class. Create a `canRecharge` mixin that adds a `recharge()` method. Mixin this into `Robot` and call `recharge()` on an instance.

**Solution:**

```
class Robot {
   constructor(id) {
     this.id = id;
   }
}
let canRecharge = {
   recharge() {
     console.log("Recharging...");
   }
};
Object.assign(Robot.prototype, canRecharge);
const r = new Robot(101);
r.recharge(); // "Recharging..."
```

**Explanation:** The robot now can recharge thanks to the mixin.

**Exercise 5:**
**Task:** Create two functional mixins: CanEat and CanWalk. Use them to create a Human class starting from a basic Base class.
**Solution:**

```
const CanEat = (Base) => class extends Base {
  eat() {
    console.log("Eating...");
  }
};
const CanWalk = (Base) => class extends Base {
  walk() {
    console.log("Walking...");
  }
};
class Base {}
class Human extends CanWalk(CanEat(Base)) {}
const h = new Human();
h.eat(); // "Eating..."
h.walk(); // "Walking..."
```

**Explanation:** Human extends Base with both CanEat and CanWalk functionalities.

**Exercise 6:**
**Task:** Create a canDrive mixin with drive() method. Apply it directly to an object instance car (not a class) so car.drive() works.
**Solution:**

```
let canDrive = {
  drive() {
    console.log("Driving...");
  }
};
let car = { brand: "Toyota" };
Object.assign(car, canDrive);
car.drive(); // "Driving..."
```

**Explanation:** Mixing into an instance object gives car the drive() method.

**Exercise 7:**
**Task:** Create a `canCode` mixin with a `code()` method. Create a `Developer` class and add `code()` to `Developer.prototype`. Test by creating a Developer and calling `code()`.
**Solution:**
```
let canCode = {
   code() { console.log("Coding..."); }
};
class Developer {}
Object.assign(Developer.prototype, canCode);
let dev = new Developer();
dev.code(); // "Coding..."
```
**Explanation:** Developer now has a `code()` method.
**Exercise 8:**
**Task:** Create a functional mixin `CanLog` that adds a `log(message)` method. Use it on a `Logger` class. Then create a `FileLogger` class that extends `Logger` with this mixin.
**Solution:**
```
const CanLog = (Base) => class extends Base {
   log(message) {
      console.log("LOG:", message);
   }
};
class Logger {}
class FileLogger extends CanLog(Logger) {}
const fl = new FileLogger();
fl.log("Hello"); // "LOG: Hello"
```
**Explanation:** FileLogger is Logger plus the logging functionality from the mixin.
**Exercise 9:**
**Task:** You have a `Player` class. Create `canScore` mixin that adds `score()` method and increments a `points` property. Apply it to `Player` and test incrementing points.
**Solution:**

```
let canScore = {
  score() {
    if (this.points == null) this.points = 0;
    this.points++;
    console.log("Scored! Points:",
this.points);
  }
};
class Player {
  constructor(name) {
    this.name = name;
  }
}
Object.assign(Player.prototype, canScore);
let p = new Player("John");
p.score(); // "Scored! Points: 1"
p.score(); // "Scored! Points: 2"
```
**Explanation:** The canScore mixin adds scoring logic to Player.

**Exercise 10:**

**Task:** Create a HasInventory functional mixin that adds an inventory array and addItem(item) method. Apply it to a Character class. Test by adding items.

**Solution:**
```
const HasInventory = (Base) => class extends
Base {
  constructor(...args) {
    super(...args);
    this.inventory = [];
  }
  addItem(item) {
    this.inventory.push(item);
    console.log("Added:", item);
  }
};
class Character {
```

```
  constructor(name) {
    this.name = name;
  }
}
class PlayerCharacter extends
HasInventory(Character) {}
let pc = new PlayerCharacter("Hero");
pc.addItem("Sword"); // "Added: Sword"
console.log(pc.inventory); // ["Sword"]
```
**Explanation:** The HasInventory mixin adds an inventory property and addItem() method to the class.

## Summary

Mixins are a powerful pattern in JavaScript to achieve multiple inheritance–like behavior by merging properties and methods from multiple objects into a single class or instance. Using Object.assign() or functional mixin factories, you can incorporate and reuse code across various classes or objects. While mixins can improve code reuse and flexibility, they should be used judiciously to avoid complexity and maintenance challenges.

# Understanding Method Chaining in JavaScript

### What Is Method Chaining?

Method chaining, or a fluent interface, is a programming style that allows you to call multiple methods on an object in a single line, one after another. Instead of performing an operation and then returning a new unrelated value, methods return the current object (this), enabling successive method calls directly on the returned object.

This approach can make code more concise and readable, especially when constructing complex operations step-by-step.

## Key Idea of Method Chaining

The primary idea: **Return this at the end of each method** (where this refers to the current object instance). By doing so, you can continue calling other methods on that same instance.

## Simple Example

```
class Calculator {
  constructor(value = 0) {
    this.value = value;
  }
  add(n) {
    this.value += n;
    return this; // return the current instance
  }
  subtract(n) {
    this.value -= n;
    return this; // return this
  }
  multiply(n) {
    this.value *= n;
    return this;
  }
  getValue() {
    return this.value;
  }
}
const calc = new Calculator();
const result =
calc.add(5).subtract(2).multiply(3).getValue();
console.log(result); // (0+5-2)*3 = 9
```

In this example, add(), subtract(), and multiply() all return this, making calc.add(5).subtract(2).multiply(3) possible in a chain.

## Benefits of Method Chaining

1. **Readable Code:** Chained calls can read like a description of operations to be performed.
2. **Reduced Temporary Variables:** No need to store intermediate results in separate variables.
3. **Fluent Interface Design:** Especially popular in builder patterns, jQuery-like libraries, and data manipulation tools.

## Common Use Cases

- **jQuery Style APIs:** jQuery popularized chaining: $('div').addClass('highlight').show();
- **Builders or Configuration Objects:** Creating objects step-by-step: new Person().setName('Alice').setAge(30).build();
- **Data Wrangling APIs:** Libraries that manipulate data often provide chainable methods for convenience.

## Potential Pitfalls

- If a method does not return this, it breaks the chain.
- Code may become harder to debug if the chain is very long and complex.
- Not all methods are naturally chainable (e.g., methods that must return a non-object value might end the chain).

# Multiple Choice Questions

1. **What is method chaining?**
A. A design pattern where each method returns a primitive

value.

B. A style where multiple methods are called sequentially on the same object.

C. A pattern that requires using async functions.

D. A pattern only applicable to arrays.

**Answer:** B

**Explanation:** Method chaining involves calling multiple methods on the same object in a chain.

2. **Which key practice enables method chaining in a class?**

A. Returning `this` from methods.

B. Using arrow functions only.

C. Using global variables.

D. Returning null from each method.

**Answer:** A

**Explanation:** By returning `this` from methods, you can continue chaining calls on the same instance.

**Which of the following code snippets demonstrates method chaining correctly?**

```
obj.doSomething().doSomethingElse().finish();
```

3. A. Each method returns `this`, so this is correct.

B. Each method returns a new object, so it doesn't chain.

C. Methods must be static.

D. Method chaining is not possible in JavaScript.

**Answer:** A

**Explanation:** If each method returns `this`, method chaining is achieved as shown.

4. **Which famous JavaScript library popularized method chaining?**

A. React

B. Angular

C. jQuery

D. Vue

**Answer:** C

**Explanation:** jQuery's fluent interface style popularized chaining in JS.

5. **What is the main benefit of method chaining?**

A. Slower execution speed

B. Increased code verbosity

C. More readable, concise code

D. Requires more memory
**Answer:** C
**Explanation:** Method chaining often makes code more readable and concise.

6. **If a method in a chain returns a primitive value instead of this, what happens?**
A. The chain continues normally.
B. The chain breaks because you no longer have an object to call methods on.
C. It throws a TypeError.
D. Methods automatically convert the primitive back to this.
**Answer:** B
**Explanation:** Returning a primitive breaks the chain since you can't call further methods on a primitive.

7. **Which is NOT a characteristic of a fluent interface?**
A. Methods usually return this.
B. Results are built up step-by-step.
C. Method calls form a chain.
D. Every method returns a unique, unrelated object.
**Answer:** D
**Explanation:** In a fluent interface, methods typically return the same object (this), not unrelated ones.

8. **In a builder pattern that uses method chaining, when is the final object typically constructed?**
A. After each method call.
B. Only at the end, when a "build" or "get" method is called.
C. Before any chaining methods are called.
D. Method chaining is not used in builder patterns.
**Answer:** B
**Explanation:** The final result is usually retrieved at the end via a finalizing method.

9. **Method chaining can reduce the need for:**
A. Additional helper functions
B. Variables to store intermediate results
C. Object prototypes
D. Class definitions
**Answer:** B
**Explanation:** By chaining methods, we can avoid using multiple temporary variables.

10. **If a class method must return a computed value (not `this`), how can we still preserve chaining for other methods?**

A. It's impossible.

B. Return `this` anyway and ignore the computed value.

C. Provide separate "getter" methods that do not end the chain.

D. Chainable methods should not return computed values directly.

**Answer:** C

**Explanation:** You might separate "getters" from chainable methods, or structure the API so that getters come at the end.

11. **Which of these is a disadvantage of overly long method chains?**

A. They are always more readable.

B. Debugging can be harder.

C. They execute faster.

D. They never break.

**Answer:** B

**Explanation:** Long chains can be harder to debug since it's less obvious where errors occur.

12. **Method chaining is often used in which pattern?**

A. Singleton pattern

B. Module pattern

C. Builder pattern

D. Factory pattern without classes

**Answer:** C

**Explanation:** Builder patterns commonly use chaining to set properties step-by-step.

13. **To support method chaining in a function-based object, what must you ensure?**

A. The function returns a promise.

B. The function returns the same object.

C. The function uses async/await.

D. The function returns undefined.

**Answer:** B

**Explanation:** Return the same object (e.g., `this`) to keep chaining possible.

14. **Does method chaining rely on arrow functions or normal functions?**

A. Arrow functions only

B. Normal functions only
C. Either arrow or normal functions can be used
D. Only arrow functions returning `this`
**Answer:** C
**Explanation:** Both arrow and normal functions can be used as long as they return `this`.

15.  **jQuery's `$().hide().show().addClass("active")` is an example of:**
A. Not method chaining
B. Method chaining (fluent API)
C. Asynchronous code execution
D. Partial application
**Answer:** B
**Explanation:** jQuery uses method chaining extensively.

16.  **If a method does not return `this`, how do you fix the chain?**
A. Return `this` at the end of the method.
B. Use `super` keyword.
C. Add a global variable.
D. Convert the method to a getter property.
**Answer:** A
**Explanation:** Simply ensure the method returns `this` to restore chaining.

17.  **When should you avoid method chaining?**
A. For simple, single-step operations.
B. If it makes the code less clear.
C. If you need multiple return values.
D. All of the above.
**Answer:** D
**Explanation:** Avoid chaining if it doesn't add clarity or if you need different return values.

18.  **A fluent interface often resembles:**
A. A chain of function calls that read like natural language.
B. A single monolithic function.
C. A global variable store.
D. A complicated nested loop.
**Answer:** A

**Explanation:** Fluent interfaces often read like sentences describing operations.

19.    **To implement a chainable method, what is the minimal requirement?**
A. Method must be async.
B. Method must return `this`.
C. Method must never do anything.
D. Method must log its name.
**Answer: B**
**Explanation:** Returning `this` is the key requirement.

20.    **Can you chain methods on built-in objects like strings by default?**
A. Yes, all built-in methods return `this`.
B. No, most built-ins return new values, not `this`.
C. Only if you modify the built-in prototypes.
D. Strings are always chainable.
**Answer: B**
**Explanation:** Built-in methods often return new values, not `this`, so they don't naturally chain.

# 10 Coding Exercises with Full Solutions and Explanations

**Exercise 1: Basic Calculator**
**Task:** Implement a `Calculator` class with `add(n)`, `subtract(n)`, and `multiply(n)` methods that return `this`. Test chaining them.
**Solution:**

```
class Calculator {
  constructor(value = 0) {
    this.value = value;
  }
  add(n) {
    this.value += n;
    return this;
  }
  subtract(n) {
```

128

```
      this.value -= n;
      return this;
    }
  multiply(n) {
      this.value *= n;
      return this;
    }
  getValue() {
      return this.value;
    }
}
const calc = new Calculator();
const result =
calc.add(5).subtract(2).multiply(3).getValue();
console.log(result); // 9
```
**Explanation:** Each method returns this, enabling chaining.
**Exercise 2: A Fluent String Builder**
**Task:** Create a StringBuilder class. It should have
append(str), prepend(str), toString() methods.
append() and prepend() should return this.
**Solution:**
```
class StringBuilder {
  constructor(initial = "") {
      this.value = initial;
    }
  append(str) {
      this.value += str;
      return this;
    }
  prepend(str) {
      this.value = str + this.value;
      return this;
    }
  toString() {
```

```
    return this.value;
  }
}
const sb = new StringBuilder("Hello");
sb.append(" World").prepend("Say:
").append("!");
console.log(sb.toString()); // "Say: Hello
World!"
```
**Explanation:** By returning this, we can chain append() and prepend().

### Exercise 3: Fluent Configuration Object

**Task:** Create a Config class with methods setKey(k), setValue(v), and a build() that returns the config object. Make setKey and setValue chainable.

**Solution:**
```
class Config {
  constructor() {
    this.config = {};
  }
  setKey(key) {
    this.currentKey = key;
    return this;
  }
  setValue(value) {
    if (this.currentKey) {
      this.config[this.currentKey] = value;
    }
    return this;
  }
  build() {
    return this.config;
  }
}
let c = new Config();
```

```
let result =
c.setKey("host").setValue("localhost").setKey("
port").setValue(8080).build();
console.log(result); // { host: "localhost",
port: 8080 }
```
**Explanation:** setKey() and setValue() return this, so they can be chained.

**Exercise 4: DOM-Like Chaining**

**Task:** Create a Div class that simulates a few DOM operations: addClass(cls), setText(text), show(), hide(). All should return this except getText() which returns the text.

**Solution:**

```
class Div {
  constructor() {
    this.classes = [];
    this.text = "";
    this.visible = true;
  }
  addClass(cls) {
    this.classes.push(cls);
    return this;
  }
  setText(text) {
    this.text = text;
    return this;
  }
  show() {
    this.visible = true;
    return this;
  }
  hide() {
    this.visible = false;
    return this;
  }
```

```
getText() {
    return this.text; // ends the chain
  }
}
let div = new Div();
div.addClass("highlight").setText("Hello").hide
().show();
console.log(div.getText()); // "Hello"
```
**Explanation:** The chain is maintained until getText() is called.

**Exercise 5: Custom Query Builder**

**Task:** Create a QueryBuilder class with select(fields), from(table), where(condition), and build() methods. The first three return this, build() returns the final query string.

**Solution:**
```
class QueryBuilder {
  constructor() {
    this._fields = "*";
    this._table = "";
    this._condition = "";
  }
  select(fields) {
    this._fields = fields;
    return this;
  }
  from(table) {
    this._table = table;
    return this;
  }
  where(condition) {
    this._condition = condition;
    return this;
  }
  build() {
```

```
    let query = `SELECT ${this._fields} FROM
${this._table}`;
    if (this._condition) {
        query += ` WHERE ${this._condition}`;
    }
    return query;
  }
}
let q = new QueryBuilder()
  .select("id, name")
  .from("users")
  .where("id=1")
  .build();
console.log(q); // "SELECT id, name FROM users
WHERE id=1"
```

**Explanation:** Classic builder pattern with fluent methods.

**Exercise 6: Fluent Color Modifier**

**Task:** Create a Color class with a red(value),
green(value), blue(value), each storing the color
component, and toRGB() returning rgb(r,g,b). Make them
chainable.

**Solution:**

```
class Color {
  constructor() {
    this.r = 0;
    this.g = 0;
    this.b = 0;
  }
  red(value) {
    this.r = value;
    return this;
  }
  green(value) {
    this.g = value;
    return this;
```

```javascript
  }
  blue(value) {
    this.b = value;
    return this;
  }
  toRGB() {
    return `rgb(${this.r}, ${this.g},
${this.b})`;
  }
}
let color = new
Color().red(255).green(100).blue(50);
console.log(color.toRGB()); // "rgb(255, 100,
50)"
```

**Explanation:** Each setter returns this, allowing chaining.

**Exercise 7: Chainable Timer Setup**

**Task:** Create a Timer class with setHours(h),
setMinutes(m), setSeconds(s) methods and getTime()
method. Chain the setters.

**Solution:**

```javascript
class Timer {
  constructor() {
    this.h = 0;
    this.m = 0;
    this.s = 0;
  }
  setHours(h) {
    this.h = h;
    return this;
  }
  setMinutes(m) {
    this.m = m;
    return this;
  }
  setSeconds(s) {
    this.s = s;
```

```
    return this;
  }
  getTime() {
    return `${this.h}:${this.m}:${this.s}`;
  }
}
let t = new
Timer().setHours(10).setMinutes(30).setSeconds(
20).getTime();
console.log(t); // "10:30:20"
```
**Explanation:** Another property-setting fluent interface.

**Exercise 8: Fluent Math Wrapper**

**Task:** Create a FluentNumber class that starts with an initial number and has methods double(), increment(), and decrement() all returning this. Provide value() to retrieve the final number.

**Solution:**
```
class FluentNumber {
  constructor(num) {
    this.num = num;
  }
  double() {
    this.num *= 2;
    return this;
  }
  increment() {
    this.num += 1;
    return this;
  }
  decrement() {
    this.num -= 1;
    return this;
  }
  value() {
    return this.num;
```

```
    }
}
let fn = new
FluentNumber(5).double().increment().decrement(
).double().value();
console.log(fn); // ((5*2)+1-1)*2 = (10)*2 =20
```
**Explanation:** Methods return this, enabling chaining.
### Exercise 9: Chainable Logging
**Task:** Create a Logger class with info(msg), warn(msg), and error(msg) that log to console, and return this. Add a done() method that returns nothing (ends chain).
**Solution:**
```
class Logger {
  info(msg) {
    console.log("INFO:", msg);
    return this;
  }
  warn(msg) {
    console.warn("WARN:", msg);
    return this;
  }
  error(msg) {
    console.error("ERROR:", msg);
    return this;
  }
  done() {
    // ends the chain
  }
}
new Logger().info("Start").warn("Be
careful").error("Error occurred").done();
```
**Explanation:** Chaining multiple logging calls before calling done().
### Exercise 10: Fluent Array Wrapper
**Task:** Create an ArrayWrapper class that holds an internal

array. Methods: push(item), pop(), clear() all return this. toArray() returns the array.

**Solution:**

```
class ArrayWrapper {
  constructor() {
    this.arr = [];
  }
  push(item) {
    this.arr.push(item);
    return this;
  }
  pop() {
    this.arr.pop();
    return this;
  }
  clear() {
    this.arr = [];
    return this;
  }
  toArray() {
    return this.arr;
  }
}
let aw = new
ArrayWrapper().push(1).push(2).pop().push(3).to
Array();
console.log(aw); // [1,3]
```

**Explanation:** Methods mutate the internal array and return this.

# Summary

Method chaining creates fluent interfaces where multiple method calls can be combined into a single expression. By ensuring that each method (except the final "getter" method) returns `this`, you can create APIs that read elegantly and reduce boilerplate. Although method chaining can improve readability and conciseness, it should be used judiciously to avoid overly complex chains that are difficult to debug.

# Conclusion

Congratulations! You've reached the end of the **JavaScript Handbook: Object-Oriented Programming (OOP)**. By now, you should have a comprehensive understanding of the principles and techniques behind object-oriented programming in JavaScript.

You've learned how to create objects, harness constructor functions, leverage prototypes, and utilize ES6 classes to build sophisticated, modular code. You explored encapsulation, inheritance, and polymorphism, as well as advanced techniques like method chaining, mixins, and the nuances of JavaScript's prototype chain. Through multiple-choice questions, coding exercises, and hands-on examples, you've gained the skills necessary to write cleaner, more maintainable, and scalable JavaScript applications.

Mastering OOP is a transformative step for any developer. It provides the structure needed to build larger, more complex applications while promoting code reusability and simplicity. By learning how to work with objects, constructors, and classes, you've equipped yourself with the tools to become a more effective and efficient programmer.

This book is only the beginning of your OOP journey. As you continue to build your skills, revisit these concepts and apply them to real-world projects. The knowledge you've gained here will serve as a foundation for your development career, especially as you work with modern frameworks like React, Angular, and Vue.js.

Remember, the best way to solidify what you've learned is to build, break, and fix. Keep coding, keep exploring, and keep creating.

Thank you for being a part of this journey, and may your OOP skills power your success in the world of JavaScript development.

# About the Author

**Laurence Lars Svekis** is a distinguished web developer, sought-after educator, and best-selling author, renowned for his profound contributions to JavaScript development and modern programming education. With over two decades of experience in web application development, Laurence has become a leading authority in the field, empowering a global audience with his clear, insightful, and practical approach to complex coding concepts.

A **Google Developer Expert (GDE)**, Laurence is celebrated for his work with **Google Apps Script**, where he creates innovative solutions for automation, workflow optimization, and custom app development. His expertise extends beyond Google technologies, with a deep mastery of **JavaScript, object-oriented programming (OOP), and front-end web development**. This unique combination of skills allows him to deliver comprehensive courses and resources that simplify even the most challenging programming concepts.

Laurence has educated over **one million students worldwide** through his interactive courses, books, and live presentations. His approach to teaching revolves around simplicity, clarity, and hands-on learning, making advanced topics like **object-oriented programming (OOP)** in JavaScript accessible to learners at all levels. His content is enriched with real-world examples, coding exercises, and projects designed to solidify key concepts.

In addition to his online courses, Laurence is a prolific author. His books, such as the **JavaScript Handbook: Object-Oriented Programming (OOP)**, offer readers an immersive learning experience with practical coding exercises, multiple-choice quizzes, and detailed explanations. These resources serve as an essential guide for both aspiring and experienced developers seeking to master **OOP principles like inheritance, polymorphism, encapsulation, and method chaining**.

Laurence's impact on the developer community is immense. As an active participant in the **Google Apps Script and JavaScript developer communities**, he regularly engages with learners, shares insights, and fosters collaboration among developers. His ability to bridge technical complexity with clear, step-by-step guidance has made him a trusted voice in the world of **JavaScript education**.

Passionate about solving real-world problems through code, Laurence continues to push the boundaries of modern development. His expertise **in JavaScript** is especially relevant in today's landscape of modern frameworks like **React, Vue.js, and Angular**, which rely heavily on OOP principles.

Through his **books, courses, and live presentations**, Laurence inspires developers to unlock their potential, refine their skills, and achieve career success in the fast-evolving world of software development. His influence extends far beyond traditional teaching, offering a fresh perspective on how education, development, and innovation intersect.

To learn more about his work and discover a treasure trove of free resources, visit BaseScripts.com, where his passion for teaching, coding, and community building continues to shape the next generation of developers.